Adventures of a Traveling Dog Salesman

Convoy To Alaska

Book 6

Published by Alaska Adventure Books

Clam Gulch, Alaska

www.AlaskaAdventureBooks.com

By Matt Snader

Table of Contents

The Snader family took the majority of the pictures in the book. However there are some exceptions. My apologies for any that I missed.

Photo credits:
Some of the house construction photos were taken by Ben Shaw and Dan Zimmerman. I have not made notes who did what. If you see a nice house construction picture just offer a hearty congratulations to both of them.

Page 51-Missie Yoder
Page 65—Paul Weaver family
Page 67-Paul Weaver family
Page 69-Paul Weaver family
Page 71-Paul Weaver family
Page 73-Paul Weaver family
Page 78-Emanuel Esh
Page 79-Emanuel Esh
Page 80-Emanuel Esh
Page 105-Leon Beachy
Page 134-Makayla Weaver
Page 137- bottom picture-Andrew Stoltzfus
Page 147- Richard Stauffer
Page 155-Marlin Swarey family
Page 177-photo provided by Gareth Byers
Page 179-Leon Beachy
Page 185-Leon Beachy
Page 187-Jerry Martin
Page 188-Jerry Martin
Page 190-Jerry Martin
Page 199-Luis Yoder

Introduction

This book is number six in a series written about our family's adventures in Alaska. I will not go into much detail about the past books, as you will just have to read them. In a nutshell, I work for an advertising company that does a lot of work with the website LancasterPuppies.com. This is where the "Adventures of a Traveling Dog Salesman" part comes in. The limo is used to advertise another site, AmericanGunDogs.com. Both sites are owned and operated by Online Advertising, LLC. We have seven children, ages 1-13. You can read my wife's side of the story in her cookbook, which is Book 4 in our series.

We struggled a bit deciding what to name this book. Marlene (my wife) audaciously suggested *The Year of TOO Much Fishing*, however this lighthearted suggestion was passed over because I personally thought we didn't go fishing enough. During the past summer we had many visitors. I wish we could name them all, but that is impossible because I already forget many names. For this I apologize and recommend you come again. Several folks have brought vehicles of their own custom design. One family retrofitted an old bus with a bathroom, kitchen and sleeping quarters. Another family retrofitted a regular enclosed trailer with sleeping and living quarters. Sadly, no one has yet driven up with a limo to visit.

Has anything worth writing about even happened in this book? You, the reader, will have to be the judge of that. I sincerely hope you don't fall asleep while reading. A lot of things have occurred in this book that I believe are at least somewhat interesting reading. Hauling 20 dogs to Alaska, the boat engine blowing up, and on another occasion the boat started on fire are just a few of the happenings.

There were also some incidents while hunting; one in which a bear actually got shot. The limo also took its turn for excitement and broke down. One late night my pickup gave out and required me to walk six miles through the dark Alaskan wilderness, unarmed. Then there were other vehicle problems which occurred in Chicago. Chicago claimed a transmission, and also caused problems with a trailer, which may have fallen apart anyway. Our new house was finished, but not without going over budget and causing all kinds of problems. I also nearly electrocuted myself with some faulty wiring.

Some folks you have read about in previous books have also moved to Alaska in this book. Andrew and Tabitha Stoltzfus moved up in May of 2017. My brother-in-law Paul Weaver (whose family visited in Book 3) talked his family into moving up after an eccentric lunatic offered to buy a house for his family to live in. Marv and Andrea Hostettler also moved back to Alaska; after a brief, and not well thought out, move to Colorado. And, of course, Dwight and Kristin Wenger have been in Alaska since 2016. Thanks to all these folks moving in, a new church was started which we call *River of Life Fellowship*. It is currently a house church, meeting in my basement.

Remember the alleged Bigfoot-plagued, abandoned ghost town of Port Chatham? Paul, Leon (from Buckeye Puppies) and myself make the 110+ mile round trip voyage in my boat to check it out. We found the shores to indeed be sinister and foreboding, or was that boring? You will have to read the chapter and find out. Sadly, no Bigfoots were sighted. Or, maybe that was a good thing.

We also, finally, got the miserable behemoth of a boat, the *Doesn't Leak*, out on the water. This is the horrible 28 foot boat that I hauled to Alaska in 2015. For the first time since I bought it, almost two years later, it got off the trailer. The boat left and returned to the dock on its own power. Everyone that finds out about that feat is amazed.

I hope the first few chapters are not too fragmented, as it is not entirely in chronological order. It was a little bit of a challenge to pull everyone's experiences together in a neat tidy document; as well as follow the various events as they were unfolding. Happy reading!

-Matt Snader, Clam Gulch, Alaska

This picture was taken by Trista Beachy at the top of the Fuller Lake's trail. In the background is Skilak Lake.

Foreword
By Josh Snader

The other day my brother called me. "Hey, I ran into some trouble," he said. With Matt, running into trouble can happen literally or figuratively. This time it happened literally. "I've accidentally overloaded the cargo trailer that Emmanuel Esh is towing. He's in Chicago and can't tow it any further because the wheels are rubbing the frame rails." This did sound like a bit of a problem. I knew where this was going, and it involved me driving into Chicago, something I enjoy as much as pulling splinters out from underneath my fingernails. Sure enough. "Could you deliver a new trailer to Emmanuel? He's on the outskirts of Chicago. I'll shop for the trailer; you just have to pick it up and take it to him."

Matt had moved permanently to Alaska and was in the process of getting all his earthly belongings from Pennsylvania to the Promised Land. I could no longer needle him about being only half Alaskan. He wasn't able to tow everything in one trip, so he had convinced other people to tow cargo trailers up to Alaska on separate trips. This left Matt sitting in Alaska with a bunch of his stuff, and his former friend sitting broken down and lonely in Chicago. Somehow, surprisingly, something went wrong with a trip Matt had planned. "Either I overlooked the trailer weight rating or the trailer shrank once it was in the sun for a few days sort of like clothing does when it's been washed with hot water." We both agreed that was probably just the hot summer sun, not that either of us had any experience with trailer engineering, or washing clothes, for that matter. I reluctantly agreed to do it, mostly out of compassion for Emmanuel and his wife, Miriam, sitting in Chicago.

I only live about three hours from Chicago (not far enough), and so I was Matt's best bet at rescue. In retrospect, I should've held Emmanuel hostage until all my demands were met. Missed opportunities aside, Matt went about searching online for trailers to buy on a weekend at a moment's notice while being in Alaska. For some reason, he wasn't very successful. Emmanuel ended up finding a much heavier cargo trailer on the other side of Chicago, so I quickly stopped communicating with Matt and found Emmanuel to be much more helpful.

Emmanuel had dropped the broken trailer in a truck stop parking lot and had picked up the new one. All we had to do now was meet Emmanuel at the truck stop and tow the broken down trailer home to my in-law's farm with my father-in-law's Ford F-350 farm truck. My wife and I jumped in the beater truck and strapped the baby seat on the bench seat in between us. Then, we headed to Chicago on our goodwill mission. Unfortunately driving a heavy duty farm truck for 3 hours is like riding a jackhammer through a speed bump factory; it's not what I would call a smooth ride. In fact, every time I drive that truck I recommit to losing weight since you can feel every extra pound of fat jiggle like Jello.

We arrived at the truck stop and quickly spotted the stricken trailer. Now all we had to do was simply unload the entire 24' cargo trailer, and then load it all back onto the heavier trailer that could handle the weight without limping along like a lame duck.

It soon became apparent why the other trailer refused to go further. Matt had boxes and boxes full of books, flooring, tables, chairs, desks, a few elephants, circus tents and several crates of what was probably bowling balls or engine blocks. We finally got everything loaded into the new trailer and sent Emmanuel and Miriam Esh off towards the sunset with a sweaty handshake and warm wishes.

We drove the jackhammer truck home again with the stricken trailer behind us. Once all the weight was out of it, it actually towed just fine. I suspect the axles were most likely a little bow legged after the experience. Since I live in the middle of Goshen, I had little room to put a 24' trailer while it waited to find a new home. So the plan was to leave it sit behind my in-law's chicken house until a new owner adopted it. My in-laws were a little suspicious of this plan since many other "sick" cars found their way out to the back 40 and ended up succumbing to their injuries and becoming a permanent part of the farm's skyline. Matt bribed me with a share of the proceeds from selling the stricken trailer. Turns out selling a lame trailer is sort of like selling a lame horse; no sane person wants to buy it.

I have to admit, when Matt told me how much the first printing of his first book cost, I thought he made a horrible mistake. I felt bad for my brother since he was going to be living under a bridge for the rest of his life. Now I'm writing the foreword for what I think is the sixth book in the series, so I'm willing to admit I was obviously wrong. In fact, I can't count the number of times I did an estimate for a customer (I do estimates for Elmer's Services, a horizontal drilling company in Howe, Indiana), and they stare at me funny the whole time I'm there. Just before I leave, they casually ask, "Is your last name Snader?" Then they practically burst with exhilaration when I grudgingly admit that I'm Matt's brother. Matt's books are certainly making their way into people's lives.

I do appreciate how my brother has pushed me to think outside the box. He's a great guy and has given me a job several times and advice on countless other occasions. Granted, most of the time I take his advice and then run as fast as I can to the most stable person I know and get their advice, just so I can balance the teeter-totter of wisdom. Of course, Matt is the one with the mansion in Alaska, so maybe I should've taken his advice more often. However, it's safe to say if I was too devoted to the comfortable bubble of normal, my wife and I would never have taken the biggest steps of our lives into mission aviation. On November 16, 2017 we joined MMS Aviation out of Coshocton, Ohio.

MMS Aviation is a Christian nonprofit group that teaches apprentices (such as myself) how to repair and maintain missionary aircraft while working on actual airplanes from mission groups from around the world free of charge. MMS Aviation has saved aviation missions over one million dollars in labor costs in 2016 alone while giving the next generation of missionary mechanics hands-on training. My goal is get my FAA A&P license while achieving 4,800 hours of hands-on mechanical experience. After the mechanical training is complete, we'll move to Burlington, North Carolina where we'll undergo pilot training for 2 ½ years with MAG (Missionary Air Group). Once that is done we'll finally be qualified to join an aviation mission such as JAARs or MAG, or 150 other missions that use airplanes in their work. We're very excited about this calling in our lives, and while God is responsible for our path in life, I like to think that my brother has given me motivation to not let normal be my expectation in life. Follow our journey at our support blog: snaderflyby.com.

That's enough about us! Matt said I could put that last part in there, and I appreciate that, Matt. Now stop reading this boring foreword and start reading this shiny new book fresh off the presses!*

*Note from Matt: I apologize to you folks finding this book one hundred years later covered with dust in a used book store somewhere.

Chapter 1
The House

In our last book we make mention of a house-building project under-way. This project started out small and innocently enough. First, we bought some land closer to town, with electric grid access. We toyed around with the idea of just setting a mobile home on some concrete blocks. I found some nifty doublewides online that advertised, "free shipping anywhere in the US." When I called for some more information, they had the audacity to say that they didn't ship for free to Alaska! That is what I call false advertising. When I finally did find doublewides in Alaska, they were very pricey, not to mention ugly-looking. I guess shipping mobile homes to Alaska gets expensive. Insulated shipping containers looked like an attractive option, but that idea was frowned upon by Marlene.

Our next plans were to have Dan Zimmerman install a foundation in the spring of 2017. As mentioned in Book 5, Dan called me one day and said he had some room in his schedule that fall already. He also pointed out if we put the house foundation in the following year, it would have to wait until early summer. This was because the dirt road leading to our land could not take heavy equipment traveling over it until it was completely thawed out. I didn't really like the idea of waiting that long, so I gave Dan the go-ahead.

One of the problems with installing a foundation is that you need a blueprint, and we didn't have one. So I quickly threw a design together. I knew that squares and rectangles are the cheapest shapes to build, so I basically stuck two rectangles together and told Dan to have at it. He obliged and did the excavating in short order. Marvin Schrock's crew did the concrete work and subfloor. The foundation cost more than I expected, but I figured the worst was now behind us. The rest of the house would go fast, and maybe even be cheaper than I was figuring. Perhaps I would hit it off with the lumberyard folks, and they would give me some astonishing discounts.

Our first plan with the house was to build as we could afford it. We would buy some lumber here, a window or two there, salvage materials off Craigslist, and after many years of labor we would fasten the last board, stand back, and admire our handiwork. Perhaps we could even hand saw the boards from the trees on our own land. Then Marlene made her remark about wanting to burn down the cabin. This was bad enough, but then she started talking about just moving back to Pennsylvania. I realized that if I wanted any hope of staying an Alaskan resident, I had better act quickly.

We talked again with our house designer, and he cobbled a design together. He did grumble a little about having the foundation already done before he started drawing up the house design. It does put some restraints on

Above: Our house foundation with subfloor installed, ready for framing.
Below: Marlene resisted my efforts to save money by buying a used trailer and just installing it on the foundation for the time being.

the design work. Here we ran into our first sign of problems. Initially we had decided to do a rancher. One floor, over a basement, and as cheap as can be. Then we decided to reserve the basement for the church to use, which meant we wouldn't want any rooms in the basement. This squeezed the main floor a bit.

The problem this created was that you can't just tuck an extra room on top of a rancher. But with the size of our foundation, a full two story house would border on enormous. So we decided on a Cape Cod style with a hip roof. This gives a little over half a story on the second floor. (Later we discovered a full two story would have been cheaper.)

After we had our design put together, we decided we might as well get a few quotes on the house. What if I went to the bother of building it myself, only to discover a builder would have done it for a lower cost? I talked to Marvin Schrock and a few other builders, but none of them could start framing before June. This wasn't fast enough, but I didn't have any other options.

One day in January or early February I called Dan Zimmerman with a question about the driveway. While talking to Dan I made the comment that I couldn't find anyone to start framing the house soon enough to suit our schedule. Dan said he might be able to help, and he would give me a call back shortly. Sure enough, when he called back he proposed that he, Ben Shaw (the fellow with the sinking boat in Book 5), and their boys would build the house. They could start in two weeks. I personally didn't see any issues with this, although it would have been nice if they could have started right away. I asked Dan if he thought we could move in by June 1st. He thought this was a bit optimistic, but we made it a goal to shoot for.

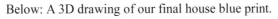
Below: A 3D drawing of our final house blue print.

Chapter 2
Matt Buys a Gulf Stream

Some folks pretended to be horrified when they heard I was looking for another RV. After my wild success with the $2,500 Mallard motorhome in the previous book, how could I resist trying the whole system over again? Except this time around I was going to keep the new RV and sell the old 38 foot Fleetwood. This did seem like selling off a member of the family. Never get emotionally attached to your vehicles, or you may find yourself doing unreasonable things.

I still wish I would have kept my dad's 1974 Ford Econoline van. Because at the tender age of 16 I was constantly pulling the engine or transmission out of my old, worthless excuse for a Mustang, I ended up driving my dad's van most of the time. I think my dad's van could even outrun the Mustang. The van was definitely sportier. Sadly, this van ended up in a junkyard. One reason I still have 'Ol Blue (the 1984 Dodge with bullet holes that I picked up for $400 in a previous book) is that it reminds me of that old Ford van. 'Ol Blue even has a manual transmission, just like my dad's old brown van. But enough nostalgia, or I'll have everyone reading my book in tears. Even worse, I might cause a surge in old rusted-out van sales, which could drive the price of my next vehicle up.

Since this was going to be my third RV, I considered myself an experienced, savvy buyer. I would know to look for holes in the roof, body panels falling off, rust holes and that sort of thing. No more Mr. Nice guy either. I would ask hard-nosed questions like, "Has this thing ever been wrecked?" or "Ever change oil?" After asking these questions, I would drive the price down to where the seller was in tears. If they refused, I would walk out, only to have them shout after me that they would accept my lower priced offer. Of course, there could be exceptions to this treatment. There were times, for example, where I would feel sorry for the person selling a product, and then I would just pay full price to cheer them up.

We were back in Pennsylvania, once again. This time was different, however. Our cabin was going to be cleaned up and sold. After this, it was all Alaska, all the time; barring those important book signings in places such as Florida, of course. Because we were selling our cabin, we decided it would only make sense to haul everything we could out of it and up to Alaska. Part of the reason for the decision to sell was the skyrocketing cost of our new house underway in Alaska. The other reason was, well there wasn't another reason. On to the next subject.

So we felt it was now time to go RV shopping. Now I know, it looks bad to complain about how much our house cost, and then go out and look

Above: Our 2001 Gulf Stream. If only it had wings and jet turbines! Oh well, it's pretty nice the way it is, although the exterior is a bit dull. Below: The inside of the Gulf Stream.

for a motorhome. But our house went so far over budget a few cheap RV's thrown in the mix didn't seem to make much difference. It was kind of like getting a heart transplant, then fretting over the costs of mints in the hospital cafeteria.

One evening I was looking over Craigslist, and I happened upon an RV ad that looked like a scam. It was a 2001 Gulf Stream Motorhome for $7,000. It had over 90,000 miles on it, which I didn't consider worn out. Best of all it appeared to have a Ford V-10. The earlier Ford chassis motorhomes, including our Fleetwood, had 460 cubic inch V-8's. These engines were serious gas hogs. Of course any motorhome will guzzle gas, but some slightly more so than others. I called the fellow, named Mike, and to my surprise he didn't sound like a scammer. I made a time the following day to meet with him and see just what he had for sale.

Again, to my surprise, Mike turned out to be a real person. I half suspected I would find out someone was just playing a joke and sending me on a wild goose chase. In fact, once my brother-in-law Paul put a sign on my Mustang advertising it for $500 (this was before he was my brother-in-law; we go way back). Later I ran a newspaper ad advertising goats for $20 each with his phone number. In hindsight, that may not have been the most mature way to handle that situation. He claimed his phone rang so much he had to turn it off for a week, while I might have had a total of three phone calls from the Mustang sign, and those callers were obviously tire kickers. This was not the yellow Mustang GT pictured in Marlene's cookbook. This was the pre-dating Marlene mustang.

The way Mike had described the motorhome on the phone, I half expected it to be in terrible condition. It did have some issues but none that couldn't be lived with. The bathroom floor was spongy, and later I found out the shower leaked water all over the place. I suspect those two issues may have been connected. Mike also mentioned the roof had leaked at one time, but the previous owners had fixed it. However, he wasn't sure, and even suggested it might need a new roof in the near future. Mike didn't have a ladder handy, and there wasn't one on the motorhome, so I figured the roof would be fine. I did poke it from the bottom side, and that was all firm. Mike did say that he had tried to seal up the roof with some aftermarket sealer. But, he complained, that product was inferior and mostly blew off. "It just doesn't stick to the rubber roof like it should," he said.

Mike went on to tell me the engine was probably shot. I thought I was hearing things. "These Ford V-10's are shot at 100,000 miles," he said. This was a bit of a dilemma for me. I certainly didn't want him to think the RV was worth a lot more than I wanted to pay for it, but I didn't want to be like the man in Proverbs 20:14: "It is naught, it is naught, saith the buyer: but when he is gone his way, then he boasteth".

Also, Proverbs 20:17 came to mind: "Bread of deceit is sweet to a man; but afterwards his mouth shall be filled with gravel."

I told Mike I thought a Ford V-10 would go longer than 100,000 miles, but he wouldn't hear of it. He insisted the engine was probably soon going to go out! When I started it with the intention of pulling it front a few feet he cautioned about letting it warm up a few minutes before moving it. "Those V-10's you need to be careful with," he said. I thought about the V-10 in my white Ford van. It had over 230,000 miles on it with no overhaul. At least 4,000 of those miles was from lugging that ugly, monstrous, and very heavy boat to Alaska from Pennsylvania. Most of the time it was badly overdue for an oil change and low on coolant. I gave up arguing with Mike. There was no convincing him that his motorhome engine wasn't on death's doorstep.

Actually, the motorhome looked pretty nice. There really wasn't much to complain about, so I asked Mike if he would take $5,000 for it. I pointed out that if the roof did need to be replaced, it would cost about $2,000 to install a new roof. What I didn't tell Mike was that if the roof ended up leaking, it was unlikely I would actually fix it. Mike looked contemplative, paused, and said, "Today is your lucky day. I feel like selling this to you for $5,000. I had offers for more months ago, but I'm tired of it in my driveway." This delighted me because I had noticed he was looking like he might have needed to be cheered up. After he accepted my offer though, he looked happy again, so it must have been my imagination. In a strange twist of fate, in an earlier book I mentioned buying a Gulf Stream being a future goal. At the time I meant a Gulf Stream jet, but hey, I'll take what I get.

After doing the paperwork, we made the drive back to Snyder County. The RV drove very nicely but had some awful rattles in it. It also seemed to wallow like a walrus in ten foot waves when you went over big bumps. The brakes were crisp though, unlike our Fleetwood. With our old motorhome, stopping was sometimes a real challenge. Another peculiar thing with the Gulf Stream was the entire front end was made entirely out of cheesy fiberglass and plastic. A moose or deer would probably sail right through the windshield, killing the driver and half the people onboard. This seemed like a serious safety flaw. You can't put a dollar value on your family's well-being, so I decided the safety flaw had to be addressed.

I called several welding shops, and none could give me a straight price on a practical, workable moose guard. All of them acted like they had never heard of such a project! Then I had a stroke of inspiration. What I wanted was nearly the same as the moose guards on semi trucks. If I could find an eighteen wheeler moose guard, I figured it wouldn't be too hard to install on an RV. An Ebay search revealed a used Peterbuilt moose guard, located near Reading, Pennsylvania (remember we were in PA for a few weeks). They wanted $600 but accepted my offer of $450. It spited me to spend so much extra money, but $450 won't even get you the time of day in an ER room. I figured it would be money well spent.

After some good-natured pleading and tasteful begging, Arlan from Clark Hill Service center agreed to install the moose guard for me. I pointed out this wasn't just some cosmetic nonsense, like fixing rust holes. And who ever heard of a mechanic begging and pleading a customer to leave? This was a matter of safety! People can get killed by flying moose! While it was at Clark Hill I also got new shocks installed. This noticeably stiffened up the suspension, making it much more controllable while driving over bumps in the road. Keeping up with the safety theme, I also had Arlan install some LED light bars. Even with my nice guard, I still wanted to avoid hitting moose.

Arlan's assistant, Ryan, was the one that actually performed the welding. He made a small subframe that attached to the frame, which allowed us to pivot the guard down to change oil and check engine fluids. I was pleased with the result. However, the motorhome still seemed to be missing something. The look was kind of a cross between a vehicle that retired folks might drive and some wild-eyed truck driver from the Yukon. There was certainly a few additional cosmetic tweaks needed, but just what, was eluding me at the moment.

Chapter 3
The Roof Blows Off the Gulf Stream

Standard procedure for Alaska trips is hauling trailers north to resell. In the past I had purchased my trailers from a place in Georgia called Colony Cargo. These trailers proved to be of good construction, with good prices and service. One day I was browsing online and came across some other trailer companies in Georgia. Their prices were less than Colony but not by a large margin. Stupidly, I decided to take a chance at one of these cheaper trailers. The particular trailer I ordered happened to be red. This should have been an omen to me, as my big ugly boat is red, communists love red flags, and also Benedict Arnold wore red. So learn from my mistake, don't buy red trailers.

The day came to pick up the cheap trailer, and Marlene and the family joined me in the motorhome for the 850 mile trek to Georgia. It was still cold in Pennsylvania, but the further south we drove the warmer it became. This seemed of no consequence, and we could drive with the windows open, which is always fun. I couldn't get the generator to start, so I didn't bother with the AC roof units.

As we merrily cruised along the interstate, I heard a thump. With seven children around you hear thumps pretty often, so I didn't pay any attention to this. Soon there was another thump. After a few more thumps I finally inquired who was banging around in the motorhome. As usual, everyone acted like it must have been someone else. So, I kept driving. Before long there were many thumps, and it became obvious that something on the outside of the motorhome was thumping up and down on the roof. Once I had the awning unfurl on the Fleetwood while cruising at 65 mph. It spread out like a parachute, causing much alarm. I wanted to avoid repeating anything similar, so I took the next exit. The next dilemma was the motorhome did not have a built-in ladder, resulting in me not being able to see what was going on. I found a mound of stone to park beside, and from a vantage point on top I could see some sort of material coming loose. The thought of the roof peeling back was a bit concerning. A GPS search revealed a Wal-Mart about five minutes away, so we slowly drove over to it. There I purchased a ladder and climbed up on the roof. I was greeted with a terrible mess.

Some genius had stuck tar paper all over the roof! Tar paper has a sticky side, and the previous owners must have thought this was meant to stick on motorhomes. In case you are not familiar with the basics of home construction, tar paper is purchased in big rolls and put on your house roof. Shingles or tin is then nailed or screwed on top of the tar paper. Tar paper is not meant to be a covering in itself, although you might not know that if you

Above: The roof peeling off the Gulf Stream! The warm weather in Georgia made the problem worse. Below: The awful El Cheapo* Trailer.

*The actual brand name was not El Cheapo but should have been.

only spend your time in rural Alaska. And it is certainly not meant to be a covering on a moving vehicle.

The warm weather on the RV roof had slowly softened up the tar paper, which is why the problem had not occurred earlier. My only option at this point was to attempt to remove as much tar paper as I could. With this completed, we went on our way. Several more times, after hearing repeated thumping sounds, I had to pull over and take tar paper off the roof. I kept reminding myself I had gotten a good deal on the motorhome anyway, but it was a bit disappointing to have the roof come off. Even stranger still, it looked like someone had tried painting the tar paper.

When we arrived at the El Cheapo discount trailer outlet, it was bustling with activity. Apparently there are many folks out there as ignorant as I was, snapping up cheap, worthless trailers. At least the service was fairly quick and friendly. However, the first failure of this trailer happened right in the dealer parking lot. The foot for the trailer jack did not fit on properly. After the folks who brought my trailer out struggled with it, I told them not to worry about it. It seemed like the issue was simply the hole in the jack's post was not large enough, and I reasoned I could just drill a bigger hole in it at a later date and slip the foot on. This idea was foiled later in the day when the jack bottomed out while making a turn at an intersection. The bottoming out action crumpled the jack like a soggy pretzel.

I noticed the sides of the trailer also flapped like oversized aluminum cans when you bumped them. After this I told Marlene that we should not haul anything very valuable in the trailer. Initially I was going to haul our kitchen in this trailer, but I decided this trailer couldn't be trusted. This proved to be about the only wise decision I made involving this horrid excuse for a trailer.

Surprisingly, we made it back to the cabin in Pennsylvania without the sides falling off the trailer or some other calamity occurring. But then we made a mistake; we started packing things in the enclosed trailer. Would the trailer make it safely to Alaska? Would it even get halfway there? These were questions I should have asked myself. But I figured, "Hey, it's a new trailer. What could go wrong?"

Chapter 4
The Reinfords Visit Pennsylvania

In our second book, you readers may remember that we stayed at the Reinford's place for what seemed like half the summer, until our cabin construction progressed enough to live in. To clarify, it did not feel like half the summer to us, but it probably did to them. We owed them a debt of gratitude for their tremendous generosity. I was delighted and a bit surprised when Twila announced they were going to be attending a wedding in Middleburg, Pa, of all places!

Naturally, I immediately invited them to stay at our place for the night or nights. They said they would, if it wouldn't be too much of a bother. I assured them it certainly would not be! They came for only an evening and a day, but it was delightful to be able to repay a small bit of their kindness.

Marc and Dorcas Yoder, from Soldotna, Alaska, also stayed at our place for a night (on a different date). I forget the occasion why they were in Snyder County, but we had a good time while they were there. Marc is a manager at Northstar Metals, located in Soldotna. Our new house has metal on the roof from their company.

Thinking back over the last several years, it is shocking how many times we have visited with Alaskans in Pennsylvania. It almost seems like everyone has a relative, wedding or some kind of family event there. Maybe sometime, once we regain our financial moorings, we will buy a cabin in Snyder County, Pennsylvania.

Chapter 5
Eskimo Checkers

Previously, I mentioned our kitchen and needing to haul it to Alaska. Some might argue that it would have been better to just buy a kitchen in Alaska, and if we were ever crazy enough to build another house I don't think I would haul the kitchen 4,000 miles. The reason we did decide to haul our kitchen such an outrageous distance was because I have a friend who runs a cabinet shop. His name is Ethan Zimmerman, and his shop is Kenton Chair Shop in Delaware. We toured Ethan's shop last year, and I was very impressed with the craftsmanship his company had to offer. So much so I decided to just order the kitchen from him and haul it to Alaska.

People that know me well will wonder when I started to care about quality wood craftsmanship. After all, my current desk is just some glued together flakeboard. My wooden gun racks were the cheapest ones for sale on Amazon, and my fish-cleaning table is made out of an old pallet. The answer to this question is simple. Let me ask you a riddle. Who spends the most time in a kitchen? And another question: Who might be the less enthusiastic member of the family when it comes to living in Alaska? Ah, yes, the answer is Marlene! Now, I must quickly say that Marlene said she would have been happy with a cheap kitchen from a big box store. She did not demand, or even request, a custom hardwood kitchen. We have lived in a long string of houses with lackluster kitchens. The first house we bought had a kitchen that looked like it was cobbled together out of old metal roofing.

I decided that Marlene deserved a nice kitchen for a change. Also noteworthy is that the kitchen plans were drawn up and set in motion at the start of the house construction, before the entire cost of the project was realized. Had the kitchen decision been made at the end of the house building process, it would have been thrown out, along with the drywall and siding (the drywall and siding had also been arranged in advance). After the house was done, and I told people our house cost more than I expected, they would laugh as though I said something hilarious. Unfortunately, I didn't realize before starting the house construction that there is apparently some kind of law of nature that projects of this type run over budget. Being blissfully ignorant of this allowed me to commit to the kitchen before it was too late to back out.

Interestingly enough, the parts of our house that could change during the construction project did. We started out with plans of fancy simulated wooden garage doors. That turned into plain white garage doors. Originally we planned for some nice wooden tongue and groove accents on some interior walls. That went the way of the buffaloes pretty early on in the game. The lookout tower over the garage was also axed very quickly. The indoor, multifloor sliding board? Not a chance. The indoor shooting range? Let's not even talk about that.

Enough whining about the cost of the house; more sordid details on that later. We are thankful for the house (hopefully when you read this we are still living in it and not on some street corner). All this to point out the connection with Ethan and his woodworking shop, which brings us to Eskimo Checkers.

One day, while the kitchen work was in process, Ethan emailed me a design for a wooden board game. Initially I wasn't very excited about it. Soon, I received a full prototype in the mail. It did look pretty impressive, being made out of furniture grade wood. It sat on my desk for awhile until we took it along on a vacation weekend with Shannon and Ann High. Paul and Jo were also along on this short trip. It seemed everyone thought we were committing ourselves to an endless voyage into the depths of space, beings as we were going to sell our property in Pennsylvania. The end result of this was a mad dash of tearful visitors, cabin trips and family reunions in the waning weeks of our stay in Pennsylvania.

During that weekend we played some games. At this point I pulled out Ethan's game, and we took turns playing it. It really was a lot of fun! In fact it was by far the most popular game that weekend. We didn't have a name for the game, and as we played we brainstormed what we could call it. Ethan had suggested Cabin Fever Tonic, but I didn't think that had a good ring to it. Paul is the one that suggested Eskimo Checkers. "It seems like a game Eskimos would play," he said. I made some graphics with that theme in mind and liked it. The decision was made to label it Eskimo Checkers. Later I discovered that Alaska Natives actually do have an old folk board game that is strangely similar, but not exactly the same. I was also a little worried that Native Alaskans would find our board game name offensive, but they didn't seem to mind. Maybe I should have just called it Mennonite Checkers.

Note: Not all the Eskimo Checkers games are made in Alaska, however, some are. This label is on the Alaska made games. All of the games are made in the USA.

ESKIMO CHECKERS

For Two Players

Object: To finish a straight row of 4 game pieces with the same characteristic

There are eight possibilities.
A winning row can be any of these:

1. All tall
2. All short
3. All dark
4. All light
5. All square
6. All round
7. All have plain tops
8. All have drilled tops

**Eskimo Checkers is a trademark of
Alaska Adventure Books**

To start:

One player chooses a game piece and hands it to the other player, who places it on the board. That player then chooses a game piece to give to his opponents. The play continues in this way until a winning row is formed or all pieces are played.

The player placing a game piece can change its position until he hands a game piece to his opponent.

The winner starts the next game by handing the other player the first game piece.

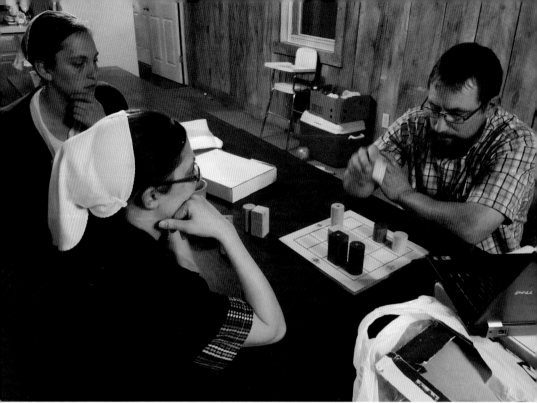

Above: Playing Eskimo Checkers at Fred High's cabin in central PA. Below: I tried to pose the children and a dog sled with the game, but it didn't work out so well.

Chapter 6
Paul's Lunatic Landlord

This year my brother-in-law Paul, whose full name is actually Paul Harvey Weaver, decided to move to Alaska. Years ago I would proudly tell people that I knew Paul Harvey. Paul is also my cousin, and growing up, he was almost like a brother to me. Paul's wife, Jo, is also Marlene's sister. Rumor has it that I caused some consternation on Paul's side of the family, but I view this as preposterous. The rumors go as far to allude that I actually talked the Weaver family into moving to Alaska. It is true I may have exerted a tiny bit of influence. For example, I think the one year we may have sent their family a Christmas card with a picture of some snow on it.

I would also point out that simply giving someone a laundry list of facts about a topic is hardly salesmanship. Imagine you and a friend were walking across the Sahara desert. You come across a person staggering along, dressed in rags, and with no supplies. It is high noon and the sun is beating down. Your friend offers this wayward hiker an ice cold glass of water, but not before giving him a brief sermon on the health benefits of proper hydration and drinking alkaline water from melted glaciers. As the dried up traveler hastily drinks your cold alkaline glacier water, you would be unlikely to tell your friend, "Wow, you're quite the salesman, talking that guy into drinking alkaline, melted glacier water!"

The situation with Paul was similar. I simply pointed out that if Paul moved to Alaska, for a mere $40 (or whatever paltry amount a resident hunting license cost) he could hunt caribou, moose, bear, deer, and a host of other animals. If he paid $5 and entered into some tag drawings, he could also perhaps add sheep, goats, muskox, bison and elk to the list. He could fish for halibut and salmon all he wanted to, for an additional $30 or so. To top it off, he wouldn't pay any state or local income tax, his income would go up (wages are higher in Alaska), and he wouldn't have to endure heat wave after heat wave every summer. Zoning hardly exists, vehicles don't need to be inspected, and license plates don't expire. Sales tax is limited at $40 (even on brand new vehicles), and guns and ammo are sold at almost every grocery store. There is also the PFD fund, which pays out typically $1,000 every year to every member of the family.

To ensure Paul had a proper understanding of marine wildlife, I also tried to send him every picture of every fish I caught in Alaska. This wasn't to persuade him to do anything, but rather to contemplate the beauty of nature, and to be glad he wasn't born on, say, Mars (I have heard that fishing is terrible there). Of course, not everyone is called to Alaska, and I do admire folks who have enough self-restraint to burden themselves with the yoke of

Paul's new house in Alaska. It doesn't look bad, and more importantly, is located only a few miles from the Kenai River and Skilak Lake. Something no house in PA can offer at any price!

civilization in the lower 48. It would be a mess up here if everyone suddenly moved up.

Paul and his family had almost decided to move, but they ran into resistance from people in Pennsylvania (a common problem--sort of the crab in the bucket mentality). For example he owed one fellow money (he didn't tell me who). This person told Paul he had better pay him back before he moved. Other folks attempted to lure Paul to stay in Pennsylvania by renting him a cheap house. Yet other people attempted to line him up to teach school. Someone called and tried to talk him into running their grocery store. It was like an all out feeding frenzy, with nearly every person Paul knew attempting to either force him to stay, or bribe him to throw away a promising future in exchange for cheap goodies and trinkets.

Paul wasn't sure what to do, his main concern being housing. He wasn't really in a position to buy a house, and he didn't have a job lined up in Alaska. Then, out of the blue someone emailed Paul pictures of a house, and said this house was under contract, and this individual hoped they would consider moving into it. The house looked promising in the pictures, and the investor even agreed to hold it for them without a security deposit. When Paul asked the landlord questions about the house, the landlord said that he hadn't actually seen the house in person. He found it on the Internet and bought it that way but was sure it would be wonderful. After all, a picture is worth a thousand words. But Paul also needed to find a way to pay back the loan in order to not really upset the person insisting he either stay in Pennsylvania or pay the loan back before moving. Suddenly, Paul got a job offer from Marlin Eicher building sheds and installing garage doors. This took one item off the list. A day later someone offered to loan Paul his needed ransom to get him out of Pennsylvania.

Finally, Paul and his family came to grips with the obvious: They should just move to Alaska. Another strange twist of fate came into play. I was storing one of my Colony Cargo trailers at Paul's place. My intention was to haul it to Alaska for resale, but I wasn't sure how I was going to get it there. I was relieved when Paul said he could just pull it for me behind his Suburban, since they were going up that way anyway.

Paul's family intended to head out Saturday, April 29. We would have loved to leave the same day as them, however my cousin Alissa Sensenig was getting married that weekend. Our plans were to attend the wedding, then leave Sunday evening. But this is getting ahead of the game.

Chapter 7
Luis and Shelly Come to Pennsylvania

These events do blur together a little bit. I'm not 100% sure where along the timeline of events we picked up Luis and Shelly at the airport, but it was obviously before we left for Alaska on May 1st. In fact it was several weeks at least before we left. Originally Luis and Shelly were going to drive down to Pennsylvania and visit Shelly's family, who lived somewhere close to Pennsylvania or Maryland. After that they were going to help get a dog trailer ready to transport our dogs up to Alaska and pull it up with their vehicle. The only problem with this well-laid plan was that we had a collection of vehicles that needed to go back up to Alaska. We had the white E-350 Ford van, the RV, the Limo, and finally an AWD Chevy van that I had picked up cheap on craigslist. I have learned if you see an AWD or 4x4 van for sale cheap, you buy it as fast as possible. They are hard to find and very nice to have in Alaska.

I offered Luis and Shelly free plane tickets to PA, if they would drive one of my many vehicles back up in our little convoy. After some discussion, they agreed to this plan. It also had the fringe benefit of shocking their family when they showed up several days before they were expected. They kept the same departure date, but simply flew instead of drove.

Luis and I discussed various ways to transport the dog sled team, which consisted of 16 Malamutes, Siberian Huskies and various mixes with Arctic bloodlines, to Alaska. These dogs had received some training in Pennsylvania already. And, yes, they were licensed in Pennsylvania, however we have not bothered to license them in Alaska (No dog licenses required in Alaska!). Luis had spent a season or two working as a dog handler for Mitch Seavy, the multiple Iditarod champion.

We talked about using an enclosed trailer, however in May it has the potential to get quite hot in some parts of the lower 48. In the odd chance we ran into higher temperatures, the dogs would overheat quickly. The only way around this would be extensive modifications to the trailer. Another idea was to buy a horse trailer and build dog boxes inside it. In the end we decided to go this route, as it provided a lot more flexibility. In the event we ever wanted to use it in the winter, which hopefully we will, it would be easy to block off the openings in the side. Also, sled dogs will overheat much quicker than get cold, so it is better to err on the side of less warmth.

Transporting dogs can be a little complicated. Our plans were to get them out every few hours so they could stretch and eat. We did not have enough room to tie all 16 dogs out at once, so we would put half of them out, feed and water them, give them a few minutes to stretch their legs and then load them up again. We were also worried about crossing the border, even though we would have all the required paperwork, including veterinarian signed health certificates. Sure, we took Noodles (our little beagle mix dog) through a few times, but that is a far cry from showing up with a trailer load of dogs.

The fine-looking dog trailer, fresh from West Virginia.

Chapter 8
Green Siding and a Red Roof?

Through the process of house construction I learned many life lessons. One of these was to never, never, use color samples that you looked at only on your computer. Computer screens, web browsers and a multitude of other variables can influence the color on your screen. While we were in Pennsylvania, preparing our convoy to head North, I happened to talk to Marlin Eicher. I mentioned that we had chosen a siding color called Cyprus. Marlin had known we were going with a red roof, and he said he was surprised we would go with green siding. I asked what he was talking about, and he told me Cyprus was green. On my computer it looked brown. This concerned me a little bit, so I told Ben Shaw to call me when the siding was delivered. There was no way I wanted green siding on my house, especially with a red roof. I suspected Marlin was wrong, but an ounce of prevention is worth a pound of the cure.

I received a phone call from Ben one day. "Your siding was just delivered," he said. For some reason Ben always sounds cheerful on the phone. "Please take a picture of the siding, metal sample and gable end siding all together, and text it to me," I asked. When the picture came through, I had to struggle to keep my stomach from spewing its contents out. Not only was the siding green and somewhat repulsive, it looked absolutely nauseating with bright red roof metal. The gable ends were to get accented with brown siding. The whole works look very disturbing together.

"Don't put that siding on," I instructed Ben. "I would rather have no siding than that horrible-looking stuff."

Ben agreed it did not match. He said he was a bit aghast when he opened the box, but not wanting to offend me, he had pretended to be nonchalant about it. Thankfully Spenards Building Supply took the vinyl siding back. Perhaps they will sell it to one of those clinics where you go to have your stomach pumped, although the clinic might lose business from it. Had they not taken it back, we would have just burned the siding, stapled house wrap all over the outside and called it good. The only slight positive side to that hideous siding is it would have probably kept the tax appraiser away.

House Construction Pictures

For the sake of space, I'm going to lump a bunch of the framing, roofing, etc pictures together in a few pages. If this type of thing bores you just skip over it and accept my apologies.

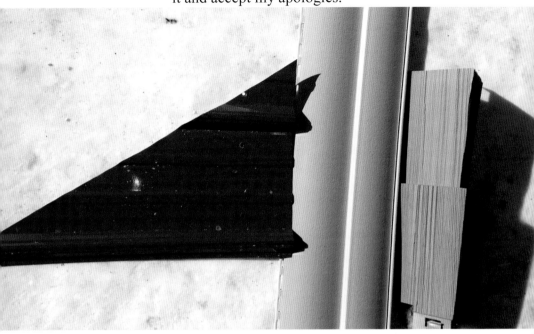

Above: The terrible color scheme I accidently picked. Thankfully it was resolved before any of the siding was installed. Below: The first floor takes shape.

Chapter 9
Matt Takes Up Weight Training Competition

As we were packing things up in PA, we had two or three weeks to go, my brother-in-law Mike Kurtz told me about a contest. He and several other guys had decided to each put $100 in a pot, and the person who lost the most body weight percentage wise in 90 days would take it all. There were eighteen people in all, bring the winnings up to $1,800. This was some serious motivation. Some people might call this gambling, but I don't, as it wasn't really chance but hard work that ultimately decided the winner. Also $100 these days won't get you much of a diet plan, especially with those fly-by-night network marketing products.

Unknown to Mike, I had spent years in training for this competition. It took a lot of work and dedication, but slowly and methodically I built up extra body weight that I could lose without harm. I didn't want to make this obvious, as then no one would want to enter a weight loss competition with me. Carefully I would sneak second helpings of dessert, snacks late at night and extra buffet trips. This also involved passing up the choicest salads, and instead going for donuts, brownies and cinnamon rolls. It also involved forgoing water, in exchange for soft drinks and milkshakes. At times I would sneak along a sugar-loaded energy drink. Often I would pass up physical work, such as cutting firewood, and instead sleep on the couch.

After about three years this hard work had paid off, and I was primed to enter a weight loss competition. Unfortunately I didn't want to raise suspicions by going around and asking people if they wanted to lose weight. Then finally, Mike came through with the weight loss contest. I almost laughed when Mike said he was going to win. He has a determined attitude and can-do spirit, but he simply lacked the raw resources to win such a contest.

The weekend before the weigh-in, I stepped up my game by hanging out at a buffet. Since the contest was announced and the contestants committed, I pulled out all the stops. From the rumor mill I heard Mike did the same thing, but as mentioned earlier he was already so skinny that he could have eaten pork rinds and ice cream the entire weekend without becoming much of a threat. The weigh-in on Monday was virtual. You simply recorded your weight and sent it in. All the contestants were part of a Facebook group, and it was here that I first got a glimpse of all the competitors. Quite a few of them looked to be no threat, but several of them looked like they had trained even longer and harder than I had. This worried me a bit. Time would tell. The final weigh-in would occur on July 3rd.

Chapter 10
Painting the RV Camouflage

One day I realized the RV should have new paint. The old paint was a bit faded, and who can stand that? After much deliberation I carefully decided what the RV actually needed was a camouflage paint job. Marlene initially was cool to this idea, insisting we already had too many camouflage vehicles. "But we only have one painted camouflage," I pointed out. "Exactly," was her response. Later though, she relented and told me to go ahead and paint it. The problem was I had too many things happening last minute; it didn't appear I would have enough time to paint it.

Suddenly, I recalled a friend of mine who painted things. His name was Jethro Horst, and he lived near Ephrata, Pennsylvania. I sent him a text wondering if he would paint a motorhome camouflage for me. A little while later he said he actually had an opening in his schedule, and he could do it. He actually acted pretty enthusiastic about it. At the last minute I almost canceled, but I figured he might be devastated, so we went ahead with the plan.

Jethro wasn't sure he would have time to finish painting the motorhome in one week, so I had several folks help out. One was Ken Martin, who is actually pictured on the cover of Book 3. Jeff Mast, who also attended Crossroads Mennonite Church, agreed to help. He brought along his brother Randy to help out. Shane and myself helped for one day, but I had too many other things to do to help much. I would have loved to help out more.

When Jethro does something, he does it right. I was startled when I noticed he had taken the moose guard off and sandblasted it. He also did some fiberglass repairs in several places, making it so you could never see it had been damaged. Picking out the paint colors was the hard part. One morning I went to Zimmerman's Paint and looked over paint samples and picked out a few colors.

The camouflage design was also a bit of a problem. I knew what I wanted, but it's hard to describe camo to someone else. One day while at McDonalds in Mifflinburg, Pa, I noticed an old camouflage pickup. I took a picture of that and sent it to Jethro. Before he started painting we also looked over camouflage patterns on airplanes and compared it to the old truck I took a picture of.

Towards the end of the week Jethro sent me a text and said the motor home was ready to go. We eagerly picked it up, only to discover that he had some awful things (and some good) buried in the camouflage design! I'll let you, the reader, see if you can discern them. Jethro said we should let the paint cure for about a month before slapping decals all over it. Because of this we ended up driving it to Alaska without our books plastered all over the side. It was still fun to drive. While not as much of an attention getter as the limo, it certainly does attract attention. It also caught the eye of the Canadian border guards, but we'll get to that later.

I thought this pickup truck was inspiring. It was parked at McDonalds in Mifflinburg, Pa.

Above: Ken Martin helps prepare the RV for painting. Below: Shane works on the RV

Above: The RV in all it's finery. The new paint certainly adds a touch of class. Below: Jethro poses in front of the finished project. He probably considers this the pinnacle of his career. Jeff and Randy Mast also helped, but I lost the picture I had of them working on the RV.

Chapter 11
Selling the Cabin in PA

Our original plan was to keep our cabin in Pennsylvania, as we have had many fond memories there. It was a special place, in part because of how we came about owning it. However, harsh financial realities dictated that we must sell it. This wasn't all bad, as trying to manage properties in multiple states can be a real headache. First, let me elaborate on how it came to be that we owned it.

Years ago we lived in Leola, Pennsylvania. Thankfully we managed to get out of there and move to Snyder County. However, our first house in Snyder County was small and over 60 years old. This place only had two acres of land, which is like living on a postage stamp. Almost none of it was wooded.

We routinely had rats move in with us, which was annoying, to say the least. Once I shot a rat in the laundry with a .22. I spent many nights sitting on the kitchen table, shooting at rats. It was hunting year round! And as far as I am aware, you don't need a hunting license if the hunt is conducted indoors in your residence. Unfortunately we never had a problem with deer getting into the house, although they probably could have slipped in if they wanted to.

The roof leaked, the septic system was a constant problem, and occasionally the wood stove would start the house on fire. One time Marlene came home with a meager bag of groceries, and I was sitting in the living room on the computer. "The house is full of smoke!" she exclaimed. Sure enough, it was. I had been so engrossed in my work that I hadn't noticed. So I got up, put out the fire and went back to work. In hindsight I should have just chased everyone out of the house, waited a few minutes to catch my breath, and then called the fire department.

The problematic septic system at the dinky hovel escorted us to the brink of bankruptcy. We were having some financial problems, in fact our only vehicle at the time was our Crown Victoria that I had purchased for $300. Just buying the weekly groceries was a stretch. Then, what should show up in the mail, but a certified letter from the township. Unbeknownst to us, the neighbor had observed some wet spots in the yard and contacted the township. In fact, I had unwittingly stumbled into a neighbor spat when we ignorantly purchased the ugliest, cheapest house in Snyder County. It turns out the previous occupants of our house and the letter-writing neighbor had fought long and hard over the septic system. It ended when the previous occupant came to his senses, declared bankruptcy and fled town.

The house sat empty for a few years, and most folks had enough sense to avoid it like the plague. Before buying the house we did have the septic tested by what must have been some fly-by-night rubber stamp con artists, who approved the septic. After getting a fraudulent bill of health, we ended up buying the house. It was priced low, after all!

The township insisted we install a new septic. No discussion was allowed on attempting repairs on the old system. When I showed them the letter from the con artist septic test, they just waved it off. I was given a brief amount of time to get an engineered new system drawn up, which cost me $2,000 just for the drawings. Originally the engineer quoted the drawings at $800, but he explained the township kept making him redraw them. At first I attempted to draw my own system, but they scoffed at the drawings.

After the drawings were done I was finally given a permit, but not before paying an additional $300. When the secretary at the township building gave me the permit, she told me I had three years to install the septic system. This was a relief! I didn't have any money, so installing it could certainly wait. Three months later, I got another very tart letter from the township. It turns out the secretary must not have told them I had three years to install the septic, and they were threatening to throw me out of the house if I did not fix the septic system immediately.

A friend heard about the whole fiasco unfolding and agreed to loan us the money for the septic. The septic was installed at a cost of over $20,000. A few months after the new system was installed, I noticed wet spots appearing in a different part of the yard. It appeared that, while driving around in a $300 car, I had borrowed and spent over $20,000 to move wet spots 100 feet to the other side of the yard (I think towards the end of this time we did pick up a van for $400). However, I'm just an uneducated pleb, so for all I know these wet spots were coming from a melting glacier.

Anyway, all that to explain why we were not entirely content with our house on Troxelville Rd. One day I listened to a sermon that said God wants us to ask specific prayer requests, so he gets all the glory when the requests are answered. Now I think this could certainly be abused and misapplied, but I didn't see any harm in trying. Marlene and I made a list of all the attributes we would want in another house, without going into crazy land. We did think perhaps we were pushing it so as it was, but the list was something like this:

- 10 or more acres
- Good cell phone service
- DSL Internet available (a bit of a rarity back in the day)
- Same school district
- Preferably not far from our old house (this was before we discovered Alaska had loose septic laws)
- Wooded land that could be hunted on
- Room for a shooting range
- Secluded
- Long lane (who wants to live next to a road, ugh)

41

- Something we could afford
- Fairly recently built (I was tired of ancient house problems)
- A septic system that worked (or at least was at least far enough away from the road that nobody would notice if it didn't)
- A Turbine Otter (oh, sorry this was a different list at a later time)

The very next day, less than 24 hours after compiling this list, we were driving back from summer Bible school. I told Marlene we should drive back Mountain Road behind Penn's Creek, just to see if something might be available. Mountain Road was connected to Troxelville Rd (where our dumpy house was along) and Route 104. Sure enough, there was a For Sale sign at the end of a lane. It was a long lane, and we couldn't see what was at the end of it. I wrote down the number on the sign, and we looked it up when we got home.

Google maps showed a house way back in the woods, and the real estate listing showed 12 acres. Best of all, it did look like it was in our price range. In fact it was well under the price we had prayed for. The next morning I called the realtor, whose name was Lynn, and he said he could show it to us right away. In fact he had just listed it that very week! We wasted no time in scheduling a showing for that afternoon.

The house was actually built and owned by someone from Lancaster County, Pa. They used it as a cabin and had built it in 1996. It was around 1,600 square feet, considerably larger than our little rat-infested hovel. We were delighted, and the thought of not living 25 feet off the road excited me very much. However, the realtor explained that while this house had just been listed, he had already shown it several times. If we did want it, we should waste no time in putting in an offer.

The problem with submitting an offer on the exquisite cabin on Forest Lane was that I didn't have enough money to pay for the house or had any financing at all lined up. That meant I would need to submit an offer contingent on financing. Offers like that are not very attractive. Lynn told me that because it was already Saturday, no offers would be shown to the buyers until Monday. He suggested I try and find the funds or financing, then submit an offer that was not contingent upon financing. Marlene and I decided this was a good idea, but I told Lynn I didn't have any money, and a bank loan would take weeks to get.

That weekend I called the same friend that loaned me money for the septic system. I explained what I wanted to buy, and the terms I could offer him (length of loan, interest rate, etc). This fellow, Bill*, agreed it was a good deal. "Go ahead and put in your offer, I have you covered," he said.

*This fine fellow's name was not Bill. I have changed his name to protect his privacy.

Lynn seemed a little startled on Monday when I put in a full price, all cash offer with no contingencies. I had thought about offering less, as all good negotiators do. However I thought the house was an exceedingly good deal, and the listing agent had mentioned he talked the owners into listing it for 25% less than they wanted to. I was concerned if an all cash, no contingency offer came through for almost the sale price the sellers might back out. But, if I gave them a full price offer, and they backed out, then they needed to pay the realtor commission on the sale anyway, as the realtor did what he was hired to do. As soon as the offer was submitted, we headed out for a business meeting in our Ohio office.

In Ohio I had terrible phone service, and I couldn't stay on top of my voicemail. When I did have service, I would frantically check my messages, but there were none about the house. Finally, after three days a voicemail came through. The sellers had finally accepted my offer. Later I heard they were very upset with the realtor and had indeed almost rejected it. I was glad I had sent it through for the full asking price.

So, we moved into the new location on Forest Lane, almost exactly three miles from our old house. As expected, the old dumpy house took a long time to sell. I ended up "taking a bath" on it, and sold it for $8,000 less than I paid for it, not including the financial devastation caused by the septic system. It was a happy day when we signed off that little shack to someone else. We celebrated by driving to Alaska, and on that trip Marlene uttered that famous, life-changing line that rocked our lives forever, which was, "I could live here".

Fast forward to 2017, when we were building our house in Alaska. That spring as we prepared to head back to Alaska with our convoy, the money kept getting tighter and tighter. We looked at many options, such as renting it out as a vacation rental. None of these were very attractive. In the past we had also looked at renting it out on a long term basis, but nothing ever worked out. About two weeks before we left I finally told Marlene, "I guess we'll have to sell this place." So we listed it with Dan Martin, a realtor who lives near Bowmansville, PA. It almost hurt to sign the paper listing the house for sale, but it was time to face the music.

Chapter 12
Getting the Dog Trailer Ready

As mentioned earlier, Luis and Shelly Yoder had flown down to Pennsylvania to help us haul our vehicles and dogs to Alaska. Initially I had thought transporting the dogs would be an easy thing and did not give it much thought. My first plans were to simply buy a 24' enclosed trailer and tie the dogs inside. The biggest problem with a setup like this is ventilation. Enclosed trailers can get hot very quickly. Also, tying dogs up in a moving vehicle is problematic. In the event you hit the brakes quickly, dogs would be flying up against the end of their leads, which could injure them. Getting tangled up was another issue. And finally, it would take too much room to put dogs on leads, unless the lead was only a foot or two long. That didn't seem like it would work.

Luis said most mushers used dog boxes, and that would be far better than trying to tie dogs up while moving. The dog boxes gave a sense of security and helped them settle down. With 20 dogs in the trailer it could get really noisy if they all barked. On the open highway this wouldn't matter, but if we stopped for gas in the middle of town, late at night, it could cause us to be very unpopular.

One day I noticed an 18' cattle trailer for sale in West Virginia. It was new and very reasonably priced. I called to get more information, and the sales fellow on the other end talked me into making a down payment. He said it was the last one he had, and of course it would take years to get another one. I secretly doubted it was his last one, but I put some money down because the price was good. Later I discovered it was actually his last one, so it was good I acted on it.

I don't remember the exact specifics, but it worked out that Luis and Shelly actually headed down past West Virginia for something. On the way back they swung in and picked up our trailer. I asked Luis if he had seen other cattle trailers there, and he said he had not. He mentioned the lot was also way back in the sticks. I suppose most things in West Virginia are back in the sticks, which is something to be admired.

After retrieving the trailer, the next step was to build the dog boxes. With time winding down, we had to hurry. I think when we started on the boxes we had about a week to get them finished. To compound the problem, we had listed our house for sale, and it suddenly appeared to be the hottest real estate in Snyder County. We did not want to complain about this, because we did need to sell the property. The realtor didn't want the driveway to look like a construction zone, so we had to try to assemble the boxes between house showings.

Outfitting the trailer with dog boxes for transporting the dog team.

One afternoon Luis and Shelly were over when I got a call from the realtor. Someone wanted a showing in the next hour. We decided to throw all the materials and tools inside the trailer, and run to McDonalds for an hour then come back. The realtor also warned us about being there when potential buyers showed up. As we frantically cleaned up the tools, plywood, and other supplies I looked at the clock. Time was almost out as we flung the last of the mess into the trailer, and quickly we jumped in our two vans and headed out the lane. At the end of the lane we met the potential buyers coming in, so that was a close call.

After horsing around at McDonalds in Mifflinburg for 45 minutes we decided to head back, only to discover that we had forgotten the van keys! Our white Ford E350 van will usually start without the keys, but not always. In our haste we had driven out the lane without the keys, only to have the van decide later that it wanted them after all. While everyone else waited I ran back to our cabin in the blue Chevy van (we had driven both vans) and got the keys, then returned to McDonalds to pick up everyone else. It does seem sometimes that we have strange problems.

Daniel Martin, our realtor, gave us a call that week. He asked me, "Are you ready to sell your house today?" In fact, I wasn't really. The house had only been listed for six days. I was kind of hoping nobody would buy it, so we could just keep it. But, that couldn't be (I know-sometimes I make no sense at all). I told Daniel that yes, I was ready to get it under contract, provided the offer was a good one. The offer was good-it was almost full price, only $5,000 less than what we were asking. Even better, it was all cash, with no contingencies on financing, and no inspections except the septic. That didn't worry me, as we had no problems with the septic. Marlene and I signed the paperwork, and six days after the house appeared for sale in the MLS system, it was sold. I felt a little numb, but it was a done deal (and remarkable work on the part of Daniel). I did have a sense of satisfaction at having sold the house for more than I paid for it, unlike the other house in Snyder County. It was here that I began to see that maybe buying bottom of the barrel junk might not actually save any money in the long run, particularly in the area of real estate.

Our "old" cabin on Forest Lane, in Middleburg, Pennsylvania will always have a soft spot in my heart. It was the first structure we owned that I didn't wish would burn down.

Chapter 13
Last Week in PA

The final sprint to our scheduled departure date, April 30th, 2017, was exhausting. On Saturday, the 29th, we had a wedding to go to. My cousin Alissa Sensenig was getting married. Alissa also worked for us for several years, which gave further reason to attend. That last week we had several friends and family come visit. Every day was like going to a funeral, with people weeping and acting like we were heading to our deaths. Personally, I thought people were overreacting at least a little bit. After all, we had already lived in Alaska and came back alive. We were simply tying up the loose ends and then going home.

That week the last of the preparations unfolded, and some complications arose. Paul was going to pull our 24' Colony Cargo trailer to Alaska with their Suburban. However, a well meaning mechanic told them they were borderline insane for even thinking such a thing. Because of this, we decided to let Paul and Jo use our white E350 van. I thought our El Cheapo trailer would not be loaded heavy. I theorized we could pull the trailer up with Paul's Suburban. Somehow I talked Emmanuel Esh, of Mifflinburg, into driving Paul's Suburban pulling the El Cheapo trailer to Alaska. He needed to wait until his chickens were out, so he would be leaving about ten days after we did.

We were to pull another Colony Cargo trailer behind our camouflage motorhome loaded with our kitchen. In the waning days I almost panicked, as I wasn't sure how I was going to fit running to Delaware to pick up the kitchen into our schedule. Thankfully my brother-in-law's dad, Harlan Kurtz, volunteered to go pick up the kitchen for us. This took a load off my mind. Harlan only charged us for his fuel, which was very kind. When I suggested he just pull the trailer the whole way to Alaska, he politely declined.

Paul and Jo were also invited to Alissa's wedding, but they were chomping at the bit to leave. Several years ago Paul had a grocery store, and he ended up closing it. The building was like a yoke of lead around his neck, and he had finally (after three years) succeeded in getting it sold. Giddy with excitement over getting rid of that building, he wanted to celebrate by heading to their new homeland. Friday evening they picked up the E350 van.

My brother Andrew, and another friend, Leroy Martin, had agreed to drive the limo. With the exception of Josh's wedding pictures in Book 3, I don't think Andrew has appeared in any of our books before. Years ago, while still living in Lancaster County we went to Churchtown Mennonite Church, which is where we met Leroy. Andrew and Leroy were going to come out Sunday afternoon after church. Luis and Shelly would also come Sunday afternoon, and we would assemble the convoy and head north. Saturday the weather was beautiful for a wedding. After the wild, maniacal last few weeks of busyness, it was nice to sit down and relax for an afternoon. At the wedding reception we shared a table with Paul's parents, Harvey and Anna Weaver. They did their best to conceal their pride and enthusiasm over Paul's family moving to Alaska. In private I'm sure their joy over this wise decision knows no bounds.

Saturday night was a furious boil of activity. We had planned to return from the wedding, nicely pack up a few odds and ends, and then go to bed, with everything ready to go the next day. However, this did not unfold exactly as planned. Remember, we had sold the cabin; nothing could stay. Everything had to go. It wasn't like we were coming back in a few weeks and could just brush things off until then. I don't know how late we were up on Saturday night, but it was pretty late, past 1 A.M.

Sunday morning rolled around, and we went to Crossroads Mennonite Church one last time before leaving. The church family gave us a blessing and prayed over us, which we appreciated very much. One lady, Lois Graybill, send a big box of presents along. We were to unwrap them at certain intervals and milestones along the way. I thought this was a very neat idea, and the children loved it. Both Grandmas also sent along some gifts and projects for the trip. Mary Alice from Crossroads also sent along some things to keep the children occupied.

That afternoon Andrew and Leroy showed up, as well as Luis and Shelly. Everyone was expecting to leave, however that was not to be. There was still rubbish scattered everywhere. The dog pens still needed to be taken down, and some furniture and other odds and ends needed moving.

Sunday afternoon our good friends Shannon and Ann High came over to see us off. They brought pizza over for everyone, which with all our belongings packed and torn apart was a huge blessing. Shannon loves fishing. I expect one day he will wake up and wonder why he doesn't live in Alaska where the fish are huge and plentiful. We can't wait until they move to Alaska. In fact, we will personally drive down to Pennsylvania with our motorhome and pull a trailer up for them for free.

Later that same evening we also ran the pathetic El Cheapo trailer down to Arlan's at Clark Hill Service Center. The plan was for Emmanuel Esh to pick up Paul's Suburban at Clark Hill, as Arlan was putting air shocks on it. The blue Chevy van pulled the trailer without much trouble, but it did seem a little swingy.

After returning we got back to loading and trying to pack the three trailers that were left in our driveway. Finally around 2 A.M. everyone went to bed except myself. I still had an article to write for the Plain Communities

Business Exchange. Finally, after about an hour that was written up. Next I went over my finances. I had pumped almost every dollar I had into the new Alaska house, and I literally didn't have enough cash to drive these three vehicles in the driveway to Alaska. Sure, the cabin in PA was now under contract, but I wouldn't see that money for at least a month. So I called up the company that holds my credit cards and had them double the limit on all of them. They seemed eager to do this, which made me feel a little uneasy!

Finally a little after 3:30 A.M. I got to bed. I was completely exhausted. The next morning I woke up around 6 A.M. and got to work taking down the dog pens. It was here I think I almost had a nervous breakdown. I was standing on the front porch and actually had tears in my eyes. I thought, "I am leaving this place and will literally never see it again!" You would think the thought of leaving Pennsylvania behind would have made me laugh uncontrollably and do cartwheels, but no, it didn't. Marlene asked me what was wrong, and I admitted that I was having serious reservations about what was taking place. I felt like what I had pushed for so hard in the past three years was unfolding before my eyes: A new "real" house in Alaska, hauling every last thing we owned to Alaska, etc, but somehow I wasn't ready for it. It also hurt to see the house I had wanted so badly a few years ago stripped bare of all the furnishings. The feeling was almost like tossing a good friend out the window and driving off.

Marlene cut through the fog with encouraging words. She could have said, "Are you insane? What is wrong with you?" But she didn't. Instead she told me that I was caught up in the moment, and what we had planned, dreamed, and yes, even fought for, was now becoming a reality. She reminded me of our future hopes, plans and dreams. This wasn't a wild impulse we thought of yesterday. Marlene was right. In hindsight, looking back as I write this, I still feel a little, tiny bit sad about selling off our Middleburg place. Also looking back I think I was reacting out of fear. Here we were, getting ready to drive three vehicles, none of which were very spry, 4,400 miles. We would be running on credit cards, which gives one a terrible feeling. Thankfully those cards have been paid back, but at the time I didn't know how that would unfold.

I had the foresight to have Marlene proofread the article I had written the night before. It was full of errors; the last half of some sentences were even missing! She patched it up, and we sent it off to the editor.

We still wanted to leave that morning, so we were busy loading and getting ready. I was in the house when Marlene said, "You need to get these people some food. Leroy is out in the yard eating dandelions!" I was horrified. Marlene was right; I hadn't paid much attention to food. I was so stressed out I didn't even care about food, but obviously I couldn't expect everyone to be that way. We scrounged up some food to offer everyone, but

Leroy said he liked eating dandelions, and that I shouldn't worry. I declined telling everyone we would be running on credit cards and at the mercy of the credit card company.

Missie Sauder also came over to help. On our trip to Alaska the previous year she had met a guy in Alaska, Luis's brother actually (Ervin Yoder), who she apparently had taken a liking to. She was planning to marry him a month or two later! Missie apparently was a low impact passenger, as I forgot she even went along until I was going over the trip details to write the book.

Finally, a little after noon we got off. Paul had some serious issues on Saturday, but I'll let you read about those in his trip blog, which I have included in the book. I also discovered Leroy was a handy guy to have a round. He carries a bunch of tools with him, and while waiting, fixed several things wrong with the limo. I was a little doubtful of my brother Andrew's ability to drive the limo, especially with a trailer, but he did fine.

We led the convoy with the motorhome, pulling a 24' Colony Cargo trailer. Behind us were Luis and Shelly, with their family, pulling the red cattle trailer with 20 dogs inside. Andrew and Leroy brought up the back with the limo, which pulled a dumpy little trailer I had picked up somewhere. I hadn't used it much, so it was anyone's guess if the wheels would stay on. About a day ahead of us were Paul and Jo and their family, driving our white E350 van and pulling another 24' Colony Cargo trailer. In ten days Emmanuel Esh would follow us up in Paul's Suburban, pulling the 24' El Cheapo trailer. With such a fine convoy, what could possibly go wrong?

Chapter 14
The Convoy Departs

Our first snag came at a truck stop somewhere in western Pennsylvania. I was inside with our family getting ready to order some fast food. I think we were at a Wendy's. Suddenly Andrew came running in (he tends to be dramatic). "The car doesn't work for Leroy!" he shouted. I had a sudden, bitter thought towards the car and went out to see what the matter was.

Leroy was at the gas pump. I was relieved he was at least not blocking traffic. Then I realized that Andrew had said, "The card didn't work", not the car. I called the credit card company and assured them we weren't trying to commit fraud, and then it worked again. Leroy gassed up the car, and everything was good again. Credit card companies love to lock up cards. I'm guessing they have a few managers in the back office who have a party all day long, randomly locking up people's cards. "Look, this guy is trying to buy a laptop at Walmart!" the one executive would exclaim. Another one would chuckle. "Not today," he would say, and with a click turn the card off. Wild laughter would sweep the room.

That evening we slept in a rest area in Ohio somewhere. Originally Luis wanted to stop like every two hours to get the dogs out, but thankfully they were traveling well and that wasn't necessary. The weather was mild and heat was not an issue. Shane discovered he could hide completely under the sofa in the motorhome, which delighted him for some reason.

Our two house dogs, Noodles and Chewy, also rode along in the motorhome. Chewy is a Cavalier King Charles Spaniel that we had purchased from Shannon High before we left. She is a nice dog and seems pretty smart. Chewy took to house training pretty well, but on the trip she started to not bother letting us know when she needed to go. After several accidents she found herself riding in the dog trailer with the huskies. These bad habits persisted, causing some domestic problems later when we arrived in Alaska.

Taking care of the dogs went pretty well. At first I was afraid it would radically slow us down, but we worked out a routine of giving them a break at least twice a day. Even though it sounds frightful to have 20 dogs in the trailer, several of them were Paul Weaver's mini dachshunds. They hardly took up any room. The boxes had solid floors and were double stacked, giving the dogs plenty of room to turn around and stand up. Each box had straw in for the dogs to relax on, and the dogs were usually quiet while driving. However, when we stopped to feed and water them it was a different matter.

The moment the dogs detected they might be getting a chance to eat and stretch their legs, they would erupt in an explosion of barking, howling

Above: Leroy fuels up the Limo at a rest stop. Below: The 32' motorhome and 24' enclosed trailer made for some interesting moments in gas stations.

and general mayhem. It sounded like a wolf pack or two in the last phases of killing a moose. I expected of course they would do this while fueling up at crowded gas stations full of noise-sensitive people (bark, not kill moose). Thankfully the dogs were pretty smart and would not get worked up unless they heard the trailer door open.

Probably the most stressful time feeding and exercising the dogs came somewhere in Indiana. We drove for what seemed like hours, without finding a secluded spot. I always thought of Indiana as being somewhat rural, but we must have hit a bad stretch. Finally we found a large parking lot and parked in the back. It was around 2 A.M. when we started getting the dogs out. Across the parking lot was a development, and on all sides there were buildings, some of which looked like apartments. In the dead stillness of night the dogs seemed extra loud. Nobody told us to leave, but I suspect the next day there were rumors circulating of wolves in the neighborhood. Driving through Indiana I noticed the roads were extra rough. I didn't give it much thought at the time, but later I did.

Below: A sight to make your blood run cold-the Canada border crossing. Sometimes they are very friendly; other days you wonder if you are going to get handcuffed and beaten.

Chapter 15
Detained at the Canadian Border

In the past few years I have crossed the U.S./Canada border at least 20 times. Once, in the limo we were searched, but it was uneventful. Several times we had to go inside and wait a few minutes, but that was the extent of our border crossing complications. I assumed this time would prove to be uneventful and had not even given it much thought. Several variables conspired to turn this typical non-event into a near disaster. I was concerned about our trailer load of dogs and had carefully gotten all the paperwork in order.

The many border crossings had lured me into a sense of complacency. In the past I would put a list together of the ammunition I had along and make careful note of anything the Canadians might be concerned about. You can't get into trouble for anything you declare, but they might keep anything they don't want you to have. If you don't declare something illegal or regulated, then you have some big problems. Previously the guards had totally ignored my detailed ammunition list, and instead of even looking at it they would just scribble some notes down and wave us through. This led me to mistakenly assume that ammunition didn't actually matter much.

As soon as we pulled up to the border crossing I realized we might have some trouble. I was following the limo in the RV, and noticed they directed Leroy to pull off to the side (always bad). When I pulled up to the booth, they started asking about the camouflage vehicles, if we were running together, and so on, instead of the usual drill. The questions seemed more pointed, and the guards didn't seem as friendly as they normally are. This concerned me, and I started to feel worked up. When they asked if I have anything to declare, I told them I had ammunition along. They persisted and asked how much ammo, what it was for, and so on. My mind went blank. I told the guard I actually wasn't sure how much ammo I had along. I told them "at least 1,000 rounds" of various calibers. They carefully made notes and told me to pull off and park beside the limo.

Luis and Shelly were also told to pull off, and we all went inside to wait. First the guards went through the limo. I had put some ammo in the limo trunk, but Leroy knew about it and had declared it, so all was well. It seemed the camouflage paint jobs had really aroused some suspicion in one particularly high-strung lady, who apparently was a manager there.

After checking out the limo, they moved on to the RV and trailer. They opened up every hatch and started pulling things out. This process took some time, and finally they came inside. "How much ammunition do you have along?" they asked. I admitted I wasn't actually sure. They told me that I had declared 1,000 rounds, but by their counting they had at least 10,000 rounds of ammunition. This floored me, and I wasn't sure how they were coming up with such numbers. It turns out they were adding the ammo in the Limo to my quota, which was 2,000 rounds. I didn't think this was fair (Leroy had declared it), but that still left 7,000 rounds unaccounted for.

While I was racking my brain to figure out what was going on, and how I could have possibly messed up so badly, I remembered the .22 long rifle ammunition. Years ago I had gotten a closeout deal on a few literal buckets of .22 LR ammo. It was packed loose and in actual buckets, and stuck underneath in the storage compartment. This accounted for a large majority of the problematic ammo. It also doesn't take much room, especially when loosely packed, but under the laws of Canada a .22 long rifle shell is the same as a .50 caliber bullet (they did act impressed over my "50 cal" bullets, as they called them).

The stern border guard lady informed me that it is ILLEGAL to bring more than 5,000 rounds of ammo into Canada, and this was going to cause me all sorts of problems. This I found very unnerving. This lady also informed me that they had found a locked safe in the trailer, and I must unlock it for them. She was sure I had handguns in the safe. I assured the lady I did not have any guns along, but she seemed to think I was lying. She even asked to see my cell phone. I handed it over, figuring I had nothing to hide on it.

I searched for the safe key but could not find it. By now it was about three hours that we had sat waiting, and I told her to just drill the safe open. Some guards happily obliged and hauled the safe off to some secret chamber inside the building. The safe did worry me slightly. I couldn't remember putting anything inside, ever, but at this point I was expecting anything. After some time the high strung lady came back to talk to me. "WHY ON EARTH DID YOU HAVE AN EMPTY, LOCKED SAFE IN YOUR TRAILER?!" she asked. I told her that basically I was incompetent, and it was a miracle I had even made it this far. She seemed to agree that I had some competency issues and huffed off. Soon she returned, and said she and another guard had some things to discuss with me in a back room.

We entered a tiny, grim-looking room. It reminded me of something the KGB might have used back in the day. I sat at a tiny table, with an obvious one-way mirror beside me. I made a mental note to be extra law-abiding for the rest of my days. One guard sat in front of me, and one stood beside me. They gave my phone back and told me they had found a text I had sent indicating that I had not brought guns along. "We are convinced you are not hiding guns," they said. Wow, that was a relief. "But this ammo is a problem," they continued.

They went on to explain they were not going to keep the ammo, but would need to charge me tax on this ammunition. At this point I didn't care, as long as they didn't lock me up. I answered a bunch of questions on the value of the ammunition. It was tempting of course to give low ball prices, but I had decided it would be very foolish to be dishonest. I gave them the best answers I could. Of course, it is always a bad idea to be dishonest.

After I listed off the value of the ammo, they stood in the corner and looked it up. I could hear them saying, "Oh yes, that looks right," and so on. That was a good sign. Finally they came back and asked some more questions. I don't know if this was some sort of test, or if it was time for a shift change, but finally they said they would just let me go without paying a tax. "You can't bring more than 5,000 rounds in at once," they explained. So on the paperwork they were going to split it up. They pointed at Marlene and Missie. "Both of them officially brought in 5,000 rounds," she said. I didn't bother pointing out their math would equal 15,000 rounds, not ten thousand. The thought of Missie and Marlene toting ammunition around struck me as hilarious, but I managed to not laugh. It also struck me as odd they didn't deem Leroy worthy of having ammo. Finally, we could go back to the vehicles and leave.

As we were walking out to leave, it occurred to me they had not once looked in the dog trailer. I decided this would be a bad time to point out the inconsistency, and we left. Ironically, as often seems the case, the issue that I had worried and fretted hours over was irrelevant, and what I hadn't even thought of became the central issue.

My poor safe, with a fresh hole drilled right through the lock. The border officials did ask permission first, although it seemed like granting permission wasn't optional at the time. I totally understand their not wanting locked safes passing through the border.

Chapter 16
Running Low on Gas

Aside from my near arrest and imprisonment at the border, the trip was uneventful. One problematic issue was fuel. The motorhome, as strange as it sounds, would go almost twice as far on a tank of gas as the blue van and trailer. The limo would fall somewhere in between. This meant someone always needed gas at times other than the rest. Of course the reason the RV would go so far on a tank was because it had a massive fuel tank, not because it had good fuel mileage.

We were on the Alcan highway, and the RV was showing about half a tank of gas, which meant the blue van was running on fumes. I pulled off at a rinky dink gas station, only to have Luis fly on past. I figured he must have plenty of gas after all, so I pulled out and followed him. Soon I caught up with the limo, with Andrew driving. Andrew was driving miserably slow, so we passed him up. Luis soon disappeared out of site, leaving us in the middle.

When we arrived at the next gas station, which was at Fort Nelson, Luis was sitting at the gas station. After we stopped, Andrew didn't show up for about 10 minutes. We were starting to wonder if he ran out of gas or the car broke down, when he finally pulled in. After talking to Andrew and Luis, I got the full scoop of what happened.

Indeed, Luis was about running out of gas. He hadn't noticed that I had stopped at a gas station when I thought he needed fuel (gas stations on the Alcan highway don't always look like gas stations). Before long he was indeed running on empty. Luis figured if he sped up and got ahead of everyone, and then ran out of gas, we would stop and help him (we were in an area without phone service). Andrew, on the other hand, was also running on empty. However he decided to drive slower and conserve fuel, hoping to go further on the remaining fuel. Both ideas had good merit, and in the end everyone made it to the gas station.

We slept in Teslin at a campground for one night. This was the only place we paid to stop at on the whole trip. It was nice to unwind and take hot showers. Everyone slept in their vehicle, which was nicer than it sounds. The blue van had a nice seat that would fold down into a bed. The RV of course had a queen-sized bed, a sofa bed and a table that turned into a bed. In the limo, Andrew and Leroy took turns sleeping on the rear seat and floor.

To take care of the dogs that evening Luis and I took the blue van and dog trailer a mile or two down the road. That night the dogs were pretty quiet. I was a bit worried they would go into one of their howling spells halfway through the night. If they did go on a howling fit, I was sleeping and didn't hear it.

The next day, while still parked at the campground in Teslin I made a disturbing discovery. Readers may discern that I view banks with suspicion. Indeed, I have a dim view of them. I woke up early and checked the Wells Fargo online banker, only to discover the check I had mailed the painter for the house had been returned! Initially I panicked and figured I must have made some calculation errors and overdrew the bank account. Because I was writing out lots of checks, for hideous sums of money, this did seem possible. However, a closer examination revealed that I did not overdraw the bank account. Instead Wells Fargo had taken the check and simply returned it.

Naturally, having Wells Fargo just willy nilly return checks did not make me very happy. I quickly called them and inquired what exactly was going on. "Oh, well this check didn't fit your spending pattern, so we returned it for your safety," said the customer service lady. I told her that I did not appreciate their effort, and I viewed them as weasels. She didn't seem to like this kind of talk, and the conversation went south. The following Monday (after arriving in Alaska) I went into the Soldotna Wells Fargo, and told them I was very upset, and unless they did something quickly I was going to close all my bank accounts with them. They wrote me a nice letter of apology, but I'm sure they can't wait to return checks again when I'm not paying attention. I suspect whoever runs Wells Fargo hangs out with the people who love to lock up credit cards. Who knows, they probably have secret board games they play at their parties with the winner being the one who upsets the most people. In a 2017 national survey, Wells Fargo ranked #5 on the list of most hated companies in America. They do work hard for their reputation.

I must admit I still bank with Wells Fargo, mostly because of the free coffee in the bank foyer. The actual people inside the local branch office do seem human. Also, some folks may have noticed I am a tiny, teeny bit disorganized. Bankers are not. This causes some personality conflicts. In fact I probably wouldn't ever like banks unless they stopped tracking my balance and instead just let me write out all the checks I wanted. Wouldn't that be nice? That is what I would call customer service. A quick stock tip: If they ever actually do this, sell any stock you have with them as quickly as possible.

Stopping to feed the dogs. You have to love rural Canada-we stopped in the middle of the road! I think one car came along the entire time we took care of the dogs. You might notice the dog trailer has no license plate. We forgot to put it on, and made the 4,000+ mile trip, and crossed two international borders, without anyone noticing.

Chapter 17
Home Again!

It was sometime in the afternoon that we finally made it to the border of Alaska. Paul and Jo were still out ahead of us, but we had managed to trim their lead to a few hours. I had been hoping to catch up with them, but with the dogs and all the vehicles in the convoy we just couldn't make good enough time. As we rolled up to the Welcome to Alaska sign, Missie played a rousing song of *Alaska I'm Coming Home* on her phone. Indeed, we were coming home. We had sold everything in Pennsylvania. All our assets were with us, in Alaska already or loaded in the trailer scheduled to depart shortly. No longer would I have to endure the haunting taunts of naysayers claiming we were not authentic Alaskans (Never mind we had fulfilled the requirements of Alaska residency for almost three years already).

Our reception in Alaska was much more positive than our entrance into Canada had been. The border guard exclaimed, "What is going on here!" when we rolled up in the camouflage RV with the limo right behind us. I explained we were coming home and were enthusiastic, loyal, law-abiding Alaskans. The guard was quite congratulatory about arriving and welcomed us back. When I nervously mentioned our abundant ammunition onboard, the guard dismissed it with a wave of his hand and a chuckle. It was good to be back.

A fish and game official did ask us if we had any hunting trophies with our luggage. I explained I had a pig head in the trailer, which he noted but didn't seem concerned about. Later I realized that I had some deer antlers laying in plain view above the kitchen sink, but I had forgotten about them.

Paul and Jo arrived at their new house that evening, while we were still lagging behind around Tok, Alaska. Paul mentioned a degree of horror when they arrived at their new place and noticed it was quite crooked. It appeared the builder had cut the sides off a mobile home, threw some pieces of firewood down, and haphazardly built some sort of house on top. I assured Paul that he shouldn't worry. It's the little touches like this that give a house character.

In Tok we enjoyed some hot food at Fast Eddy's, which had been a bit scarce on the trip. I suspect Leroy ate more than one dandelion along the way. He showed me a nifty little booklet he had along that identified edible wild plants. This might be a nice cost effective way to travel in the future, although I suspect plants growing right beside the road might have a coating of oil and dust, which might mitigate their organic properties and nutritional value.

Above: Pulled off at the Alaska sign, getting ready to cross into Alaska.
Below: Josh's beard balm sticker is still on the back of the Alaska sign from the year before!

The Arctic Anabaptist

Paul Weaver (my brother-in-law) writes a blog called the Arctic Anabaptist. He does a good job of relaying their trip north, so I will include some of his blog entries. Due to time constraints I cannot include all his blogs, however the most relevant ones pertaining to the book are included. So allow a brief interruption for Paul Weaver…

The Arctic Anabaptist: Why Alaska?

Why Alaska?

This question is understandably oft asked of me and my family. It is a good question considering that our home in Alaska is over 4,000 miles from where we currently live in PA, and considering as well, the fact that nearly all of our family resides and will remain in PA. What could possibly make us pull up all our roots and head way up North? I am going to attempt to answer this question in the next several blog posts. I will answer with multiple short posts because you and I are both probably very busy and have time for only a few paragraphs at a time. (Perhaps more on that topic later.)

I have always been a bit of a visionary. Well, maybe more accurately – a wild-eyed visionary. I don't think I am a contrarian but I do tend to do things differently than the masses. Quite frankly, the masses scare me. It seems to me that when an idea is accepted *en masse* then it is probably a compromise of truth and it is time for me to head the other way. I am that way in many areas of life – not much for the status quo. The same applies to climates – when the masses head south; I love the North. I remember as a youth staring at the map and wondering if missionaries ever go north to the remote Siberian, Greenland or Canadian villages. It seemed to me that Africa, Central America, and South America – the warm climates- got a lot of attention while I rarely heard or read of anyone ministering in the Far North.

Reason #1 – Someone should go. We are willing. Why not us?

Furthermore, it seems that it is easy to plant Anabaptist churches in areas of fertile soil and favorable growing climates. Not that I am against the agrarian lifestyle, in fact, I am quite in favor of it; but the Kingdom of God should be first about fertile hearts rather than fertile soil.

I acknowledge that the vast majority of the world's population and the poorest live near the equator and that those regions should have a high priority for the advancement of Christ's Kingdom. But, at the same time, where we minister should not be about numbers and our logic; rather it should be all about obeying the will of God. How do we know the will of God? I will save that answer for the next blog.

The Arctic Anabaptist: Why Alaska Part 2:

-Did God *call* you to Alaska?

-How do we know the will of God?

The answer in short is that we can know the will of God by reading His Word. Christ's commands are to be obeyed. They are the will of God for our lives. When God says in His Word – "Go ye into all the world…"; we go. When God says, "Give.."; we give. Etc.…

But what about the specifics? How do you know God is particularly calling you to Alaska?

There are several reasons why I believe that our move is God's will for us as a family. No one reason alone is a good indication of God's will but when compiled together with lots of prayer-our faith is strengthened.

• As I mentioned in the previous post, I have often felt compelled to the North and often dreamed of moving into such a region. Does God work through these desires? Yes, I believe He does but it would be foolish to rely only on this as a sign of God's purpose for you. Selfishness is deceitful.

• Christ commands that we "go into all the world…" Alaska is certainly included in this and there does not seem to be an abundance of conservative churches present in the state.

• Circumstances, or "doors" as we often call them, have aligned in amazing ways. Our property sold within a week of when we wanted to leave. Our concerns for occupation and housing were erased. The cost of the move was covered by generous friends. Circumstances by themselves are not always direct answers of God's will, but they certainly help determine direction. My vision for my family involves a simpler lifestyle than is easily lived in more affluent areas. While most might want to avoid the difficulties that a simplistic lifestyle may present; I believe that these difficulties provide opportunity to build character in children. More on this later perhaps.…

In summary, we do not have a specific calling in regards to an exact ministry or location, but we are called to live out the Kingdom principles no matter where we are and what we are doing.

Circumstances and the inner witness both agree to us moving to Alaska; so we go.

The Arctic Anabaptist: Start and Restart

All of our plans, preparations, and packing for our move finally ended on Saturday, April 29 when we pushed, or rather, smashed our mattresses into the back of the trailer, and we loaded our suitcases into the van. After a prayer we took off, or more accurately we set forth about like a snail with an oversized shell would begin a journey from one side of a forest to another. The prayers continued on down the road (and they continued in varying fervency for the duration of the trip).

As we were packing, I knew our trailer was getting heavy when we kept finding things that would be great in Alaska, and we started having to stuff every nook and cranny so these things might fit. I had prided myself somewhat with the amount of "stuff" of which we sold or disposed, but I realized quickly that we still had too much. So we stuffed the stuff in as best we could and embarked with trailer tires bulging and the rear of the van sagging.

We had gone nearly 10 miles when we realized that something was wrong with our setup. After going over a few bumps (very, very minor bumps in comparison to what lay ahead) the trailer went into a wild swaying and swinging. This was not good! I got the rig under control, and we proceeded more cautiously to a gas station for our first of very many fill-ups. I cranked the friction sway control down very tight and thought that that should fix the swaying problem. Nope! The van and trailer still had a propensity to tango. We pulled into another gas station and made arrangements to dump more of our stuff at Jo's sister's place. We crawled our way back to their place and proceeded to unload our carefully packed trailer into their hoop barn. I rearranged some heavy pieces of stuff and left more of it behind in their hoop barn. My brother-in-law and I also worked on our weight distribution hitch and got the rig into a somewhat better condition for travel.

So we embarked again.

The Arctic Anabaptist: Learning to Drive

After casting off more of our earthly possessions we set off toward the northwestern horizon and far beyond it. We certainly moved at a faster clip than the covered wagons of old, but if compared to a wagon and team of oxen, our team had a limp.

We had a decent F-350 Ford van to do the pulling, but with the weight that we were pulling I think a semi truck would have been more in order. We seemed to have taken care of the swaying issue. but the top speed was still 55 mph. I did manage 60 mph on some stretches, but I had to be very careful especially on downgrades, and when a semi truck went flying past.

The first leg of the journey was through western PA on Route 80. That seemed to be one of more tense stretches because 1.) I was still learning how this rig handled, 2.) there were many hills, and 3.) there were many trucks. The speed limit was 70 mph for most of Route 80, so you can imagine how fast those trucks barreled around me doing a measly 50-55 mph. Perhaps the other motorists would have been more understanding if I had had an orange triangle on the back of the trailer and an Amish hat on my head.

I had to keep two hands on the steering wheel practically the entire trip but especially on Route 80. Several times I was caught relaxing or reaching for another sip of my coffee. A semi would sneak up and pass me before I noticed it. I was constantly watching my mirror so as not to be caught off-guard, but in spite of my efforts I was blown onto the shoulder of the highway several times. Something about the air turbulence of a passing semi caused our rig first to be drawn toward the passing vehicle, but then as it was almost passed, it pushed me away toward the right shoulder. The result of all that was me gripping the steering wheel and gritting my teeth as I sawed away on the wheel, trying first to avoid a collision, then next to avoid all the obstacles on the shoulder of the highway. Sometimes there was no shoulder. Those miles were even more tense.

Despite the difficulties and dangers, we kept plodding on. Our first night was spent near Cleveland, Ohio. We were completely exhausted after packing and repacking and the tense drive through western PA. We were exhausted enough to not care that the cheap motel room I found smelled like a cigar bar and the towels in it were only somewhat white. We were just praising the Lord that we made it as far as we did. Every mile seemed like a miracle.

One day down and many more to go.

The driving posture needed for the overweight rig. (Note that I am trying to smile in spite of the stress.)

The Arctic Anabaptist: Onward, Still Onward

After a good night's sleep in the dirty but cheap motel, we again began our journey with perhaps a bit more enthusiasm than the first day. I was still very apprehensive and was a bundle of nerves heading toward Chicago. Fortunately the flat roads of Ohio and Indiana were a much easier drive except for the frequent construction zones in Indiana that were a little sample of what was to come later on the Alcan highway. We made it through Chicago by Sunday afternoon and continued into Wisconsin where we found a resting place at the Orange Moose Motel. We were going to do a family picture with the big orange moose statue, but it was cold and rainy, and we were anxious to keep the wheels rolling.

Monday found us rolling through Wisconsin, Minnesota and into North Dakota. We enjoyed the many lakes along the highway through Minnesota and North Dakota, but after several hours of exclaiming over all the waterfowl the scenery all began to become a bit mundane. The rolling hills and lakes I can enjoy, but the long stretches of flat farmland had me bleary-eyed. I guess I am not much of a farmer.

The grain elevators are the most striking pieces of landscape with the exception of the tractors. The farmers out here use tractors and implements that could barely turn around in the eastern fields!

We stopped in the small town of Harvey, North Dakota at a little motel that we later found was very near the railroad tracks. I heard a train or two but after battling the rig all day, I probably could have slept through a tornado.

The next day we drove for a bit and entered the town of Portal, North Dakota. This is where we planned to cross into Canada. We were a bit unsure of how border crossing would go with such a tightly packed trailer and no passports. Our passports had not yet arrived in the mail by the time we left so we went anyway hoping to make it through. You do not need a passport to enter Canada, but you do need a passport to enter the US.

We were pulled into the inspection bay, and we had to answer lots of questions – mainly regarding the handguns that I didn't have along. They inspected my long guns and ammo which I carefully declared and filed the correct paperwork and about an hour later they let us in. We continued nearly through Saskatchewan before stopping for the night.

Saskatchewan is mostly flat as well with lots of grain elevators, trains and tractors. We found another motel that was cheap enough, that is, if I made my calculations right from Canadian to U.S, and continued on bright and early the next day. Soon after we entered Alberta we discovered that one of the trailer tires had a hernia. There was a small bubble beginning to protrude from the sidewall. We continued on to a larger town where we found several tire shops but only one that had the time to change our tire. They had a new 10-ply tire in stock and promptly went about changing it. As I was watching the mechanic struggle to lift the trailer with a 10 ton floor jack I became very thankful and apprehensive—thankful that we were replacing this tire here at the garage and apprehensive regarding the other tires and my inability to even get any of my jacks under the squatting trailer. The young mechanic asked where we were from, and I said we were from Pennsylvania. I knew I was far from my previous home when he asked, "Where is that? Is that in Canada?"

After a few more prayers of praise and even more of intercession for the tires we headed for British Columbia. We pulled into Dawson Creek later in the evening and stopped for the night at a motel that was nearly full of oil and gas workers.

Tomorrow we begin to travel the Alaska Highway!

The Arctic Anabaptist: Into the Wilds at Last!

My initial thought as we started on the Alaska Highway was that this road is as good as any other. I was preparing myself for a good 1,000 miles or more of gravel or crumpled blacktop. Fortunately most of the Alaska Highway is paved, and it has a few stretches that are smooth. The first several hours of travel were pleasant, and my confidence began to build. The first steep mountain downgrade eroded that confidence significantly. We came to a pull-off at the top of a hill that was there for trucks to pull into and check their brakes. No big deal. In the East there were plenty of places like that as well and most of the downgrades following seemed easy enough. We stopped to look at the sign which indicated the turns and grade of the hill.

There were several turns and the steepest portion was 9% grade. I kept the van in a low gear and started down. I could always feel that we were overloaded, but these steep downgrades sharpened that sense of feeling substantially. I think I could have stopped if I had so desired. I am still not sure. What they don't tell you on the sign at the top of the hill is that the road is narrow and rough and under construction!

We met quite a few trucks on the Alaskan Highway. We often met them at the times when I was frantically clutching the steering wheel and developing spasms in my leg from braking. They would calmly or not so calmly pull out from behind me and roar on past. I couldn't help but admire these truckers. My guess is they are not wearing skinny jeans. We even had a greyhound bus pass us periodically!

We now had to watch our gas gauge and plan accordingly. Throughout the trip we did not have a problem with "potty breaks" like I thought a family with six children would. One of the reasons is that we stopped so often for gas that everyone had frequent opportunities to use the washroom (as they call restrooms in Canada). The gas stations on the Alcan are further apart, and some were not open for the season when we passed through. Gas stations along the Alaskan Highway tend to be more interesting. One had thousands of hats hanging from its ceiling. Some are just shacks with fancy names.

We drove until nearly dark and decided to try sleeping in the van for the night. We looked on our Alcan map and saw a rest area a few miles ahead that had bathrooms. The only bathrooms that we found, however, were in the trees. Other travelers must have been deceived by the map as well because toilet paper was strewn throughout the branches of bushes and trees in protest.

We all found a spot in the van to sleep and actually slept well for a few hours. Exhaustion enables a good sleep even when you are cold and laying over a hard arm rest. We got an early start that morning because everyone was shivering. Fortunately daylight comes early in the North so we could easily see the random bison that wandered onto the road. (Our windshield was cracked on previous road trips through the Alcan when driven by the Snaders.)

We saw lots of bison and other wildlife along the Alcan. The scenery improved dramatically in British Columbia and the Yukon Territory. I would highly recommend the drive, but I would not recommend pulling an overloaded trailer.

Our God is an awesome God! His handiwork is evident everywhere, but through this area it is loudly proclaimed. We stood in awe at the majestic mountains, beautiful rivers and the wildlife. I absolutely loved it in spite of the stress!

Another point of interest was the Sign Forest in Watson Lake, Yukon. There are literally thousands of signs from all over the world. We saw quite a few from PA including Ephrata, Harrisburg, Lancaster, and others. I substantially expanded the hunting opportunities for the PA hunters by nailing a Pa Game Land boundary sign on a tree. (I did not steal the sign – I purchased it at an auction.)

The Arctic Anabaptist: Border, Moose, and Home at Last!

Friday evening, which was the completion of seven days of travel, found us in a motel in Destruction Bay, Yukon. I had a bout with a stomach bug and was feeling weak and tired. We had stopped to examine nearly every consecutive outhouse in an approximate 30 mile stretch of the highway. I felt so bad that I even relinquished the driver's seat for several miles. During those few miles I emptied what little was left in my stomach and felt much better. I blame the sickness on a little generic energy drink that I purchased at Watson Lake. My wife pulled into a gas station to fill up the van and to empty the contents in the trash can; I then jumped back into the driver's seat. It is not that I didn't trust my wife to drive, but I felt it was my responsibility to get my family safely to Alaska. Unfortunately, I cannot say that I drove for the entire trip; I missed about five miles.

We had an excellent night's rest at Destruction Bay and continued our trek after the sun rose high enough to warm the road. I was concerned about ice because the temperature was 24 F, and there was ice coating everything. We had driven through several snow squalls the day prior, and I just didn't want the added stress of slippery roads. By 7:30 the sun had risen over the eastern mountains, and we set off for home!

Shortly after Destruction Bay we arrived at the Alaska border. This crossing had the potential to get a little sticky. My wife and I did not have our passports or our birth certificates with us. They were probably at the Sterling AK Post Office, because we left before they arrived in the mail, and our mail was being forwarded. I needn't have worried at all. The border agent listened to my story and looked at the printouts I had that proved we had applied for passports. That was all he needed and in a matter of 5 minutes we were through! After a short visit with the US Fish & Game officers we were again rolling in Alaska! We still had many hundreds of miles to go, but everyone in the van was very excited to see our new home state at last.

The roads didn't improve in Alaska, in fact, they were worse. A driver has to remain alert for the many frost heaves and potholes that frequent the highway. These frost heaves are hard for a person who has never experienced them to imagine. With our rig they were even more pronounced, because we would get to bouncing as the van went over them, and the trailer would then give a few more bounces as it passed over.

We stopped for lunch at Fast Eddies which is a really nice restaurant in Tok, Alaska. We pressed on with satisfied stomachs and a fervent desire to see our new house.

The fun wasn't over yet. We encountered more mountains and steep grades, but these didn't seem as bad for some reason. Of course, a day couldn't pass without something frazzling our nerves. On one particular winding downgrade heading into the Mat-Su valley, we met a moose. It was an encounter that I was trying to avoid, and by God's grace we survived with nary a scratch. The roadway was somewhat narrow and had a high bank on the right hand shoulder. A moose just plunged over the bank at the precise moment we were near it. I yelled and yanked on the wheel the best I could without wrecking the van and trailer and cringed, waiting for the impact. I still have no idea how we missed each other, but as we passed I looked into the mirror, and the moose had managed to turn on a dime and was now running parallel with us. Despite their clumsy appearance it is evident that moose are nimble and quick. I was trembling a bit after all that excitement, and we praised God over and over for saving us.

The day grew very long as we traveled the last leg of the journey. We passed through Anchorage around 9:30 pm and headed down the Seward Highway with a few more hours left to travel. The daylight faded into dusk and then darkness, and we were now exhausted which made the last hour seem so very long. We saw another brown bear a few miles after Cooper's Landing and soon after turned into our new home. We praised God for the miracle of safety and good travel. I felt so often throughout the trip that I was testing Him.

We made it by God's grace!

So concludes our journey to Alaska.

Our journey of life still continues, and that too is only by God's grace and marvelous provisions. As I write this we have now lived in Alaska for about 3 weeks and are absolutely loving it! We have had many gorgeous days and are settling into our cozy home nestled in a bunch of pine and birch trees. There have been disappointments and trials as you would expect with any significant move but we feel very, very blessed.

Praise be to God! Now, back to Matt................

Chapter 18
The New House

On May 7 we rolled into the new house at Clam Gulch. We had been gone from Alaska for a few months, and the construction had continued without us there. I was anxious to see the result of the huge sums of money I had sent north. My first thoughts upon walking into the house was, "OH NO! I mortgaged my entire future for this?!!" The drywall was up but not painted. No plumbing fixtures were in, and the place looked about as cheerful as a morgue. Now, I was not expecting these things to be finished when we arrived. I am only pointing out that as we walked in, it looked awfully rough and depressing. As I walked around the new house I felt a bit of anger and resentment towards it. Thankfully Marlene said she liked the house. Outside the yard was a slog of mud, which didn't help appearances any.

We parked the motor home beside the house. Our old Fleetwood motor home was also parked there already. Andrew and Leroy moved into the Fleetwood, and Luis and Shelly headed home to their house in Sterling. The week that followed was very depressing indeed. Not only was the house a mess, we were living in a motorhome that did not have a water heater or shower. We had 16 barking dogs tied to various trailers and four wheelers in the driveway. The neighbors surely thought a family of lunatics had moved in. We don't have any really close neighbors, but we do have some that are within barking distance.

Every few days we would head up to Sterling to Paul and Jo's house to take showers. It almost seemed like building the cabin in Anchor Point all over again, except at least this time we weren't stuck in a tent. Despite Paul and Jo's house having been built without a level and tape measure, the plumbing worked well. It even featured a jacuzzi in the master bedroom. Paul reported that his landlord had been less than helpful (in fact downright surly and unpleasant) when he reported the dismal appearance of the house, suggesting that they just bulldoze it. Paul decided the rent was cheap enough that they could just put up with it.

We could have gone down to the cabin in Anchor Point, but we were anxious to move into the new house. With contractors coming and going it was easier to manage in the motorhome. Also, because of our shortfall of cash, we had decided to put the property in Anchor Point up for sale. It would be easier to show the cabin to prospective buyers without seven children running wild in it.

Andrew and Leroy helped move our furniture, vehicles and four wheelers up to the new house in Clam Gulch. Leroy proved again that he is a handy guy to have around. For some reason I lost the four wheeler key to the

Kymco. This didn't stop us from loading it, as Leroy simply hotwired the ignition.

Loading the four wheeler onto a trailer, we discovered something startling. This was the same trailer that Leroy and Andrew had pulled for over 4,000 miles the week before. The trailer had a hitch made for a two inch ball, but we had pulled it that far with a 1 7/8 inch ball. This meant the trailer had never been properly latched, and it was a small miracle that it made it through ok. Now we had a problem. We wanted to pull the trailer, but we didn't have the proper ball. When I suggested we just pull it anyway (after all it just went 4,000+ miles), Leroy said he was ok with being stupid by accident, but he didn't want to be stupid on purpose. I could see merit in that, and we waited to use the trailer until we got a proper ball.

That week the limo left Andrew and Leroy sit alongside the road. Andrew was very unimpressed, even after I pointed out it had made the initial trip back to Alaska without any problems. The problem was the same fuel pump wiring harness issue that had plagued the limo in our first and second books. Leroy managed to wire it together enough to make it back to our house, but to this day Andrew says he doesn't trust the limo. I must admit Ford could have done better with the fuel pump wiring harness design.

Andrew teaches the Limo a lesson with a well placed kick. Leroy looks on.

Chapter 19
Problems in Chicago

Soon after we arrived in Alaska, Emmanuel Esh and his wife planned to leave Pennsylvania pulling the El Cheapo trailer. Originally Emmanuel was going to drive Paul's Suburban, but Arlan at Clark Hill said this was a terrible plan that would surely result in transmission failure. Arlan is usually optimistic. If he says something won't work it's best not to try. This led us to the problem of finding a vehicle to pull the trailer to Alaska. I always wanted to have a big, hard core diesel pickup so I decided to shop around for one. This idea vanished as quickly as it started, when I looked at the prices of heavy duty diesel pickups. It seems that big, heavy duty pickup trucks come with a sizable price tag.

As the time came to leave, we came up with a new plan. Emmanuel mentioned he was open to the idea of selling his truck, which was a Dodge 2500 with a Cummins diesel. A very nice truck indeed, but it had one fatal flaw: it was 2 wheel drive. Being silly, I decided we could probably sell it in Alaska anyway, so it was decided that Emmanuel and his wife would bring the truck to Alaska, pulling our trailer. I would then buy tickets for their return flight, sell the truck and send them the money for the truck. Everyone would be pleased and happy. After we arrived in Alaska, and before they left, I mailed them my credit card to pay for their fuel on the trip up.

The evening before Emmanuel planned to leave he gave me a call. He had taken the trailer to the scales and weighed it (I didn't know anyone actually does that), and the total weight came in at 9,000 pounds. The trailer's gross weight was 7,000 pounds. I always figured that companies build a little extra margin into those weight suggestions, so I told him to just go for it. After all we almost always overloaded the Colony Cargo trailers by a few thousands pounds without any problems, and those have a gross weight of 10,000 pounds. Let's just say that it turns out El Cheapo trailers take those gross weights very seriously. If you are loaded at 7,000 pounds with an El Cheapo, you better make sure not too many flies land on it, or the wheels might kill someone as they fly off.

The first day of Emmanuel's trip went well. Then around 5 A.M. the one morning I got an urgent-looking text from Emmanuel. "Call me as soon you can," it said. That didn't sound good, but I figured the trailer was new, so that couldn't be the problem. Figuring his truck broke down, and at least that would be his problem, I gave him a call. "I'm in Chicago," he said. "And the trailer tires are scraping the fenders." My first thought was that I should have told him to go around Chicago, as nothing good ever happens there. Actually, once I did eat at a Cracker Barrel close to Chicago that had good food. But good things in Chicago are rare.

Thankfully Emmanuel found a truck garage that had time to take a look at the miserable trailer. The truck garage said the El Cheapo trailer needed new springs, as the springs were now sagging badly. After a day of running after parts the trailer shop had the trailer patched back together. What a relief! Now they could get back on the road.

The next day I got another call from Emmanuel. With the repairs he had made it about ten miles, when smoke started pouring out from under the trailer. Now the tires were not hitting the fenders, they were scraping the frame rails! It seemed with the stiffer springs, the axles had bent like wet noodles. We briefly discussed replacing the axles, but Emmanuel said the entire trailer seemed to be on the verge of collapse. When the jack was lowered to lift the trailer off the hitch, it now sagged crookedly. The whole thing was a mangled mess.

I now had $600 in repairs into a trailer that wasn't even worth the dead bugs on the roof. The only thing to do was cut our losses. But another issue arose: I didn't have any money for a new trailer. The credit card I sent Emmanuel was almost maxed out, and there was only enough room for fuel. At that point I thought of Alan Reinford. He now had a trailer shop (along with some other fellows) outside of Soldotna and was always buying and selling trailers. I called him and explained the situation and told him if he bought a trailer, I would pay the gas to bring it up. After the trailer got here, I would get my stuff, and he would get a new enclosed trailer that he could sell for a profit. Alan liked this idea and wasted no time in lining up a trailer on the outskirts of Chicago.

Somehow my poor brother Josh always gets dragged into these bizarre situations. This whole sad tale was taking place about 100 miles from his place. I called him and told him about the trailer disaster that was now unfolding. Josh graciously agreed to borrow a Ford F-350 and drive it out to meet Emmanuel at the dumpy El Cheapo trailer, which was now immobile. Our theory was that after the trailer contents were transferred to a decent, non-junk trailer, the junk trailer axles and suspension would raise enough to allow the trailer to be towed.

Because the trailer Alan located was west of the dilapidated junk trailer, Emmanuel unhooked his truck and headed west to pick up the good trailer. In the meantime Josh and Janice headed his way to meet him at the junk trailer site (Josh and Janice were coming from the east). Despite being parked on the outskirts of Chicago, nobody bothered the junk trailer. I was secretly hoping a gang would steal it, or burn it, so I could collect insurance on it. Unfortunately it was left alone.

By early evening all our personal items were loaded into the new, usable trailer. As we hoped, the decrepit, mangy, miserable excuse for a trailer

I totally hate getting texted sad pictures like this! This garage is attempting to fix the El Cheapo trailer by installing heavier springs. We discovered that is like trying to turn a skinny half dead horse into a champion racing stallion by mixing coffee beans in the oats.

After figuring in the cost of Emmanuel and Miriam's airplane ticket, paying Josh and Janice, dealing with trying to sell the two wheel drive truck, and the bath I took on the El Cheapo trailer, it would have been cheaper to pile the trailer contents in the driveway of our Middleburg property, soak them with gasoline and then torch them.

Above: Our load of garbage in the parking lot near Chicago

Left: Emmanuel and Josh sift through the sorry contents of the El Cheapo trailer. My sincerest apologies for having to deal with the mess!

straightened out once it was unloaded. Josh and Janice were able to pull it back to their place, where Josh eventually sold it to some unsuspecting poor soul. We did give a healthy disclaimer with it, but apparently someone needed an oversized trash can, or possibly used it to teach a graffiti class in Chicago.

Finally with a decent trailer in tow, Emmanuel and Miriam once again headed north. I shuddered at the thought of Paul and Jo having tried to use that trailer instead of a quality Colony Cargo one. The way they were loaded, that pathetic trailer would have probably just split in half somewhere, the smoking tires taking to the skies like rockets.

The rest of the trip went pretty smoothly for Emmanuel and Miriam, except for the border crossing. The Canadians about had an aneurysm when they heard they were pulling a trailer full of things they had not packed. They didn't have anything to worry about; I was careful to not put anything with that trailer load that would have needed to be declared. The Canadian border guard told them it was "very dangerous" to haul someone else's things. At this point, I don't think the Esh's would have argued. Finally, they were admitted to Canada, and the rest went pretty well. I did feel bad for how their trip went, and decided that I would not be buying any more El Cheapo trailers. In fact, I won't be pulling any more El Cheapo trailers, end of story. A quick suggestion for people owning El Cheapo trailers: Pull them across the border into Mexico, unhook, and then skip back into the United States.

One time I did that with some old pallets, and I got away with it. We had taken some food to an orphanage in Mexico, and the US border patrol wouldn't let the pallets back into the states. Illegal immigrants, no problem, but they stand firm on pallets. So we turned around, threw them beside the road on the Mexico side, and headed back through the US border. Nothing like committing a crime, then skipping the country. Actually, it is probably legal to litter in Mexico (judging from the streets). I'm not attempting to endorse crime. I'm sure there are many Mexicans who would appreciate an El Cheapo trailer. Boy, it is hard to stop here without going into a long bunny trail on our food-hauling trip to Mexico, but we must move on.

Right: Josh and Emmanuel finish moving the last of our rubbish over to the non El Cheapo trailer.

Chapter 20
Jerry and Marian Save the Day

Also showing up around the same time were Jerry and Marian Martin from the Penn Yan area of New York. Jerry's visit was almost an after-thought, and wow, I am glad he could come. He does woodworking and in the past has also done general construction. Jerry's dad is Ivan Martin, the same fellow who we hauled to Canada in the maiden voyage of the limo. Ivan is Marlene's uncle, and Jerry, Marlene's cousin.

In the past we had talked about Jerry and his family visiting Alaska, but it had all been just talk. A few weeks before we left to go back to Alaska, we had visited with them. The topic of Alaska came up, and I told him he might as well come up. I agreed to pay for the plane tickets for his entire family, and in return he would do some work on the house. At the last minute I almost backed out, because the tickets were more than I expected, and we needed eight of them. But, I bought them anyway. This turned out to be a very wise decision. Also we discovered that we saved about $1,500 in tickets if they would stay an extra ten days. This brought their visit up to almost a month! Jerry wasn't sure they wanted to stay that long, but after some consid-eration they decided to come for that length of time. I also agreed to pay him the difference in ticket price, figuring that the longer he was here the more work he would do.

In an extremely rare display of coordination, I managed to have Jerry and Marian fly in at the same time Andrew and Leroy flew out. When I dropped Leroy and Andrew off at Ted Stevens International Airport in An-chorage, I walked inside to use the restroom. Inside the lobby I ran into Jerry, by himself, looking a bit worked up. Here he had misunderstood the signs and walked out of the gate area by himself, leaving Marian behind with all seven children. When he tried to go back, security prevented him. This issue was soon resolved, as Marion and the rest of the family figured out where he went.

Typically when I pick someone up in Anchorage they arrive at some outrageous time like 3 A.M., and then we are driving back with one eye shut and blurred vision in the other. Jerry's had flown in around 7 or 8 P.M., giv-ing us the luxury of driving back awake. With bathroom breaks and fuel stops it was still after midnight when we arrived back in Clam Gulch. Jerry's family set up camp in our old Fleetwood motorhome. This worked out well, except for the fact the hot water heater would randomly shut off. But if all you have to complain about is cold water in Alaska, you're doing good.

The reason I shudder to think of Jerry not coming to Alaska was, I had overlooked a few things. Originally, I asked Jerry to come trim the house. The reason I almost backed out on Jerry coming was, trim is one of those things that is optional. So the house doesn't have interior trim, who cares? It's not like the insulation will fall out or the roof will leak. Other folks didn't quite see it this way, so Jerry's came. However, once they were here I was extremely, super glad they came.

I had forgotten that things like the interior doors were considered "trim". Also convenient was the fact Jerry knew how to install kitchens. Even better, Jerry is a go-getter who could zoom around Home Depot grabbing things from memory, while I would stare blankly at the shelves wondering what all the numbers meant. Typically I spend more time in and driving back and forth from Home Depot than actual time working on a project, not necessarily because I am a fast worker.

Jerry builds staircases for a living. Originally, way back, we had discussed doing a grand staircase chiseled from antique hardwoods sourced from exotic lands. In the end we simply grabbed some compressed OSB railings from Home Depot. Here was another reason that it was very good Jerry came. Foolishly I had thought, "How hard can it be to make railings?" It is not hard to make railings out of 2x4's and drywall screws, but if you want a railing that is straight, level, and not falling down, it can be difficult. I was impressed by the job Jerry did on our railings. The actual staircase was installed already, courtesy of the local lumberyard, which I'm sure only deals in the finest quality products.

The staircase railing was the first order of business once Jerry arrived. It was necessary because we discovered children have a built-in desire to jump off things. We couldn't even let the children go upstairs without someone standing guard. Even then they would take running starts towards the edge, only to be turned back by the yelling and shouting of the startled sentry. This only goes to prove my theory advanced in *No Place Like Nome*, which is, children are not happy unless they are hurting themselves. You wouldn't know this by the way they scream and cry when they do actually get it accomplished.

Above: Jerry and Marian, holding their son Benjamin. Shane and Jesse look on in the background. Below: The second floor with no railing, a true hazard!

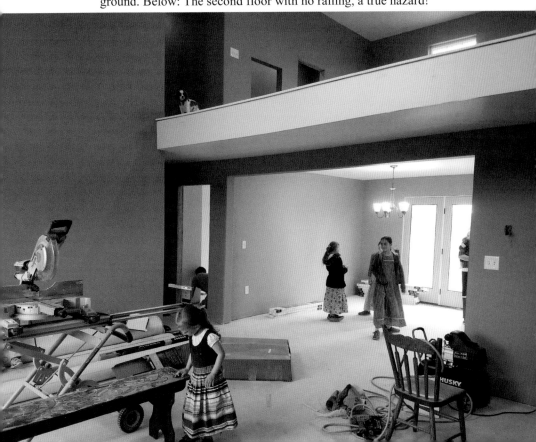

Marlene picked some less than standard color choices. It took us awhile to convince the painter this was actually what we wanted! These are both girls rooms.

Above: The house looks almost finished; all it needs is some garage doors and trim. Below: The master bathroom, still needing a vanity. This room makes me hungry for blue berries. We also have a canary yellow spare room, and a cyan laundry room!

Left: The upstairs bathroom.

Below: Jerry and Marian's twin girls, named Anita and Amanda. I would be making things up if I told you I can tell them apart.

Right: The hallway leading to the laundry from the kitchen. The door leading to the garage is on the right.

Below: This room is over the garage. Originally it was going to be unfinished, however we decided to finish it out and put the school desks and my office in it. Calvin and Jesse just finished installing the flooring before I took the picture.

Chapter 21
Matt Walks Six Miles in the Dark

Somewhere in this mix of mayhem, two fellows named Calvin Martin and Jesse Stauffer showed up to help with the flooring. Jesse helps run a flooring business near Selinsgrove, PA, called Country Flooring. Jesse is Marlene's cousin and was actually in Alaska the year before. He had driven up with John Lapp (of Plain Communities Business Exchange) and a vanload of guys. Calvin works in construction somewhere near Snyder County. Both guys were avid bikers and brought their bikes along. At first I thought this was silly, as you can buy a bike at Wal-Mart for less than the shipping to get it here. But their bikes are made out of some kind of lightweight titanium carbon fiber anti-gravity who knows what. They paid more for their bikes than I did for any of my vehicles, it sounded like. So it did make sense to bring them along.

Jesse, Calvin, and Jerry went along to Home Depot and helped me pick out flooring. This sounds pleasant and easy on paper but is very different in real life. Marlene and I had ordered some carpet a few months earlier, and it had just shown up at the Home Depot in Kenai. We also intended to pick out some flooring for the rest of the house. This turned into a mind-numbing nightmare.

It turns out there is much more to flooring than just tossing some carpet down on plywood. I was faintly aware of this, which is why I talked Jesse and Calvin into coming up to help. But oh the misery! First there is the carpet itself. Then you need to worry about the backing, tack strips, carpet stretchers, seams, and enough other things to give a CPA a headache. The calculations! We, of course, didn't want to buy too much carpet or vinyl planks. This involved careful crunching of stacks of numbers, figuring out the square footage. But it got worse than that. Figuring square footage is tough enough, but then you had to calculate the waste a roll makes, and so on. I tried to look intelligent and follow along, but I suspect I had flecks of foam coming out of my mouth by the time we checked out. It makes me wonder how many carpet installers gave up in frustration, took the easy road out and became rocket scientists.

One night I needed to run out and get some gasoline for the generator, or maybe we needed to start a campfire, I forget (those sour-faced people on the gas cans annoy me). Either way I decided to make a quick trip to Kasilof and fill the gas cans. I was on my way back with full gas cans, when I realized I missed our road. In fact I missed it by a couple of miles. So I turned around and headed back the way I had come. Suddenly all the lights in the dash of the pickup lit up. This was odd, as I had never seen this

Above: The pickup with a trailer load of carpet and padding. Many thanks to Jesse and Calvin for figuring out what we needed. Below: The kitchen waiting to be installed.

happen before. It was then I noticed the oil pressure gauge read zero. I hoped this might be a malfunctioning gauge and considered just stepping on the gas. About this time the truck shut off, and I managed to coast off the road a bit. Running an engine without oil pressure is generally not recommended, and I hoped that I had not damaged the engine. I checked the dip stick, and there was no oil on it at all!

There was nothing to do but call someone and ask to get picked up. However, when I reached for my cell phone, it was not in my pocket. Suddenly, I realized that Marlene had asked for my phone as I had walked out the door of the RV. It was over six miles back to our house, and it was now after 10 P.M. It was still May, and it was going to get dark. I hoped I could get back before dark, as I didn't have a flashlight or gun along. How silly could I have been? But it was supposed to just be a quick trip for gas, not a survival expedition. I didn't want to stay in the truck all night, and I figured it was a reasonable risk to just hike back. Unfortunately I was wearing some very uncomfortable fishing boots.

All went well until the sun set. It was so dark I couldn't read the road signs from ten feet away. Suddenly I became aware of all sorts of sinister noises beside the road. I told myself I was simply being over-sensitive, and I should just relax. At that thought there was a sudden crashing of underbrush beside the road. This was not my imagination! After some thrashing around, whatever it was ran the other way. It was probably a moose. A mile down the road this happened again, nearly giving me another heart attack. Perhaps it was good I didn't have a gun along, without a flashlight. I even tried hitchhiking. But who would pick up a hitchhiker on a deserted road at midnight with no flashlight? Had someone been crazy enough to do that, I'm not sure I would have trusted riding with them.

Finally, after several hours I tromped in our lane. It was now past 1 A.M., and I was thoroughly tired out. As I opened the door and walked in, Marlene asked where in the world I had been. As I relayed the sad tale I informed Marlene that she would be getting a phone in the very near future. She had resisted my earlier efforts to get her a phone, for reasons that remain unknown. She is a bit "old school". That is fine with me. I don't want a wife who is addicted to Facebook and the latest trendy network marketing products that make you live to be a gazillion years old (really, instead of worrying about cleanses or chemicals, wouldn't it just be easier to move to Alaska where the air is clean, and the fish are cheap?).

The next morning Jerry and myself headed out to see if we could coax the old, treacherous pickup back to life. We filled it up with oil and attached jumper cables. Finally the old beast fired up (with an extra rumble due to a loose exhaust pipe). Jerry started hollering at me to shut it off, so I quickly complied. The pickup, way back in the day, had been equipped with an engine oil cooler. Over the years the line running from the engine to the oil cooler degraded, until the evening prior it had just decided to let loose.

When the line broke, the oil pump in the engine sprayed all the oil right out the tube. Engines must have a lot of oil pressure because that morning when I started the truck, it emptied out five quarts of oil we had just added in less than 30 seconds. This is a great way to flush out your engine block but a bad way to drive around. This would also explain why the engine was mysteriously out of oil the evening before.

There was nothing to do but tow the old clunker back to the house. We connected a chain and pulled it back with the white van. Usually when I try to tow a vehicle, someone gets rear-ended or nearly killed by a flying chain, but in this case it was uneventful. The pickup ended up clogging up the driveway for almost the entire summer, until I finally figured out a fix that was semi permanent.

Below: Jerry hauls a cart of lumber and supplies through checkout. This load looks like it is for the stair railing.

Chapter 22
The Boat Motor Melts Down

In my experience, a fishing trip is not authentic unless you have some sort of disaster. It seems to be one of the laws of nature. Because I don't like dealing with big disasters, I'll frequently wait to replace a tire, as I would rather deal with a flat tire than a blown engine or a shark jumping in the boat.

Occasionally I'll not put the plug in the boat, and hope that counts as enough of a disaster so we are clear for the rest of the trip. It's a way of tripping up Murphy, so he gets confused and leaves you alone. Folks who don't understand these laws often make the mistake of thinking I'm careless, but I'm actually just looking out for their safety. If enough people practiced these safety habits, boating in general would be much safer, although perhaps less convenient.

Calvin, Jesse, and Jerry had been hard at work on my house. I decided such good workers deserved to go fishing. After all, free help has limits, which can be stretched with some fish. After this fishing trip, it is surprising they didn't just walk off the job.

Shawn Zimmerman was also along. Shawn had driven Paul's Suburban up to Alaska without incident, except for some hassle at the border. There was an upside down 12 foot boat strapped to the roof, and the border guards were almost beside themselves with worry over marine life sneaking through on the boat. Paul consoled the guards (on the phone) and assured them it had been out of water for several years, and any marine life hiding in it would be long dead. Ironically they gave me no hassle at all when I rolled through the border with my 28 foot boat. I suspect they thought the 28 footer didn't even look seaworthy, so it was the least of their worries that day.

If readers recall, the last time I used the boat was the winter before. I had taken Adam, Suni, and Josh out fishing in November of 2016. The boat had given us a good scare when the two stroke oil line broke and pumped all the oil into the bottom of the boat instead of the engine (of course it was cold, dark, and late at night). Despite this setback, we were able to improvise and limp the boat back to Homer, and all was well. This was also the same situation where miscommunication caused my dad to think our boat might be sinking and called the Coast Guard.

The broken oil line had been fixed, and the main oil tank filled with a fresh supply of oil. The 150 HP Mercury two-stroke engine also had a spare reservoir, which is what had enabled us to return to the dock. The backup tank would allow the boat to run for awhile without a supply from the main oil tank. The boat will sound an alarm if this small tank starts to run low. The only way to fill this backup tank completely is to allow the engine to run and pump it full. This takes some time, which means you must listen to the annoying alarm for a few minutes.

So it was, when we launched the boat. As we slowly crawled out through the Homer harbor's no wake zone, the alarm droned on and on. Finally, the alarm stopped. After a second or two the alarm started up again. I figured the backup tank was finally almost full, and this alarm would soon stop once and for all. It soon did stop all right, but not really in the way I was hoping.

As we pulled out of the no wake zone into Kachemak Bay the engine shut off. This didn't particularly concern me, as we were only idling along. It was not unusual to have the engine falter and need to be restarted. This time however, I only got a "click" when I turned the key. I was dismayed, as I figured this must mean the batteries were dead. They were on the charger before we left, so that explanation didn't make sense. Glancing back at the engine, I realized the batteries were not the problem. Smoke was now pouring out from the engine and engine cover, and the stench of melting plastic filled the air!

The situation was pretty self-explanatory. Because I did not have a separate heat gauge, and the alarm was beeping due to the backup oil tank being refilled I had no idea there was a problem. Avid boat users will be quick to say, "Aha! That is not true! You can watch for a stream of water spraying out the side of the engine to make sure water is being circulated."

That is true on most outboard engines, but this motor did not always spray water. It was equipped with a thermostat that turned this stream of water on and off. The thermostat had malfunctioned, cooking the engine. Hopefully you're not the type that will disagree anyway and send me angry letters demanding a correction in the next book. I frequently overhear people arguing about game laws in the store, and sometimes it makes one wonder if it will lead to fist fights.

To make our boating situation worse, we were now drifting towards a very large coast guard cutter. This huge boat (it is like 200 feet long) is almost always parked right outside the harbor and is moored on one side of the Homer Spit. I didn't know what would happen if we drifted up against this thing. They would probably mistake us for terrorists and cut the boat in half with machine guns. Thankfully another boat came by and offered to give us a quick tow out of the way and into deeper water.

Amazingly I had a kicker motor along that worked. The reason I didn't just fire it up and move was because I had to connect the fuel line and fiddle with it. After a few minutes I got the little engine fired up, and we could cruise at 5mph. Originally we were going to head down to Port Graham (over 20 miles away) for some Halibut fishing. This plan was quickly discarded, and we putted about a quarter mile out of the harbor and tried some fishing there.

Above: The turncoat 2-stroke engine that burned up, reinforcing my opinion that 2-stroke engines are only useful as boat anchors. Below: Jerry contemplates how fun it would be to rip a piston out and beat the engine with it. Shawn prepares some bait.

Above: Jesse had the whole front of the boat filled with rope before he gave up.

Right:

Calvin holds up a nice sized pollock he caught. If you enjoy fish sticks, then these fish are for you! They are a lot of fun to catch, even if they are not as tasty as halibut.

We were only fishing for a few minutes when a State Police boat pulled up alongside us. This was a bit concerning, but I was fairly sure we were current with the regulations. You never can tell, as there are so many of them. Just as they pulled alongside, Calvin caught a halibut. They politely waited until he reeled the fish in, then started asking questions. First, they informed us that they bring good luck, as evidenced by the fish. They were very easy-going, and I soon became more relaxed. They asked about the boat registration, our fishing licenses, if we had flares onboard, and so on. The only area I was lacking in was having a class 4 throwable floatation device. This is simply a floating device you toss out if someone falls overboard. I was told to get one before I went out again, and then they were on their way (I did actually buy one before going fishing again).

While we were fishing Jesse amused himself by calling boat shops and getting quotes on new boat engines. I laughingly told him to not worry about that; I was done with boating. This boat was going to be put out to pasture. I would develop new hobbies and interests on land, perhaps tending sheep. Boating was simply a fool's game with endless amounts of money being thrown overboard. Plus I knew what to expect if we installed a new outboard. Undoubtedly the next time we went out the hull would split wide open, and the new engine would go down to the bottom. It was better to play it safe.

As we fished, Jesse kept plying the phones. He put so much effort and time into comparing prices, haggling, and researching that I began to feel bad. It would be terribly ungrateful for me to just discard such hard work. Here he was, slaving away all week installing flooring and now trying to do me this other favor. How insensitive would it be to just brush it off! I decided maybe, just to make Jesse happy, I would follow up with the best priced boat shop. After all, I wasn't going to pull out the flooring after he left. Why throw out this work?

That day we caught several halibut and a few other fish. Jesse got something huge on his line that had us all worked up. After he pulled and pulled for fifteen minutes or so, he finally got it up to the boat. Instead of a monster halibut, it was a rope! What a letdown. Jesse wanted to see what was on the other end of the rope, so he pulled and pulled. After the boat was full of rope and still no end in sight he gave up and threw it all back in. Hopefully it wasn't connected to any sunken treasures or submarines. Amazingly, the kicker motor got us back to dock, and we called it a good day of fishing, even if we didn't go far.

Above: This huge special ordered roll of carpet was a real challenge to move around. Below: The house continued to look like a construction zone, which it was.

Above: No kitchen counters, no problem! We were glad though, when Sam showed up to install them. Below: Sam gets the bathroom cabinet ready for a countertop.

Chapter 23
Halibut Fishing with Professionals

The day we were out fishing, Sam Chrisner showed up with the countertops. He owns part (or maybe all, I have no idea) of TCC, also known as The Cabinet Company, or maybe it stands for The Countertop Company. Dwight Wenger graciously came over and helped carry the counter tops in. When we returned from fishing, the kitchen looked finished. Since we were using the house as we built it (something I don't recommend), we had previously fabricated our own countertops out of cardboard and plywood. Sam joked we didn't need his services, as we were able to take care of ourselves.

Notably though, he did not try to hire us as subcontractors. Because of our sad attempt at fishing I felt I needed to take the guys out again. I booked a charter with Ninilchik Saltwater Charters for the following week. They cautioned me about the tides, saying they were extra high. We decided to go anyway, because Jesse and Calvin were soon going to leave. It was like a breath of fresh air to be able to go out fishing on a reliable boat.

The day of our fishing trip, we arrived at the charter office around five in the morning. We had a seat in their office and waited for the captain to tell us to get in the van. I noticed two people calling around frantically, asking about borrowing a boat. This perked my interest, and I asked Jim, the owner, what was going on. He informed me that the boat we were taking had started leaking hydraulic fluid that very morning. Without this system they could not steer the boat. I was ok with waiting to see what other arrangements they could come up with.

Finally about an hour later they found a mechanic who could come fix the boat. He grumbled about being hustled out of bed, but the show must go on! I made a mental note never to become a boat mechanic. Or if I did, to never tell anyone about it, especially customers.

Because of the tides, the Halibut fishing was terrible. Thankfully the Kings did well, and Jesse, Calvin, and Jerry all caught nice ones. As is typical, I caught no Kings. The only King I ever caught was a small one in *The Year of Much Fishing*. It seems when it comes to salmon fishing I'm a bit lackluster.

While we were trolling for Kings, everyone except Shane fell asleep. This was due to Calvin, Jesse, and Jerry all taking motion sickness pills. One side effect was extreme sleepiness. Of course nobody thought to read the bottle before taking the pills. I didn't take any motion sickness pills, but I was so tired from all the house craziness that I could sit down and sleep anywhere, anytime. We would all sleep in the boat cabin until someone heard a reel go wild, then it was a frenzy of yelling and scrambling to get out the cabin door

Above: Ready for the tractor to push the boat into the water. Below: Calvin battles a King Salmon, which is almost ready to net.

Above: Calvin with his King Salmon. Below: Jesse with his King Salmon. Both fish were well over 30 inches long, but I don't remember the exact measurements.

for the rod. You can tell I'm a bit slower than the rest. By the time I got out the door, someone always had the rod already.

A humorous incident that occurred while fishing was a misunderstanding over a decal. Puffins are common in Alaska and are the north's version of penguins (penguins only live on the south pole). A popular way to express "No Smoking" is to have a picture of a puffin with an X over it. Get it? No puffing. Anyway, the boat had one of these stickers mounted inside the cabin. Jerry saw this and thought that puffins must be an invasive species. He asked the boat captain, Sandy, if he shoots a lot of puffins. Sandy told him he "shoots every one he sees." Jerry was left pondering this for awhile until he realized there must be more to the sticker than killing off puffins.

Jesse caught a good sized spiny dogfish shark. We had caught several of these the year before with Henry and had mixed results eating them. The charter guys didn't seem too excited about the shark, and not liking the taste of previous ones we tried, we threw it back.

The halibut fishing was miserable that day. I caught a small halibut early on (only 10 pounds), but ignorantly threw it overboard because I figured I would catch bigger ones. And so we fished and fished. Finally we gave up on the Halibut and targeted the Kings, which we did pretty well with as described earlier. It was almost time to head back, when Shane had a hit on his salmon rod.

The fish on Shane's rod behaved strangely for a salmon, and soon it was obvious we had hooked something else. It was like pulling in a boat anchor, not like fighting a wild king salmon. We started to suspect we had hooked a Halibut. Sandy helped Shane bring the fish in closer, and we all hoped the line would hold. Salmon tackle is heavy, but not nearly as heavy as the tackle used for Halibut. With the fish next to the boat, the deck hand gaffed it and hauled it overboard. It was a nice sized fish! Shane was quite

pleased. The salmon hook had almost pulled out; it was only hanging on by a thread. It was a small wonder the fish didn't escape.

With a 60 pound Halibut on the boat, we let Sandy off the hook for not catching more. Indeed the fishing is worse with clam tides. Plan your trips accordingly! And schedule your Halibut fishing before you get here. If you just arrive in the middle of July, you are unlikely to get a seat on anyone's boat.

Chapter 24
The Dog Takes up Drinking

Our one Alaskan Malamute, Denali, got loose. While all our dogs stay around, they cause all sorts of problems if they are all loose at once. So we keep them tied or in enclosures if they are not training. It wasn't a big deal that Denali got loose as she doesn't run off and is pretty mild mannered, except when it comes to killing small, tasty animals. In this case she decided to take on a porcupine. The porcupine lost the contest but not before filling the dog's mouth and snout with quills. This was indeed a serious problem. Naturally it occurred on a Friday evening, after the vet's office was closed. Later I found out they have an emergency number, but at the time I didn't know about it.

Denali acted like the quills didn't hurt very much, although surely they did. We managed to pull a few out, but she didn't appreciate this. The quills came out very easily if we could get her to hold still. What would be easy to get as a pain killer? I contemplated reading about historical civil war battles.

I headed to the local liquor store. Our church frowns heavily on humans drinking alcohol (alcoholism is a big problem up here, and we don't want to be part of the problem). However, nobody had ever expressed concerns about animals drinking (or smoking). First I asked the clerk what would be a good choice to get a dog drunk. He acted like he had a hearing problem and looked confused. After I carefully explained that I had a dog that needed intoxication, he still seemed puzzled. I'm guessing being a liquor store clerk is not high on the list for talent. Finally he suggested blackberry brandy. I wouldn't be surprised if he just recommends the same thing to everyone with dogs.

I made a custom-mixed drink consisting of part gravy and blackberry flavored hard stuff and gave it to Denali. She lapped it right up, and then sat looking at me expectantly, as alert as ever. This stuff was a joke! I thought surely I had wasted $20 and went back inside the motorhome. An hour or two later I came out to check on Denali, and she couldn't stand up straight. I quickly summoned Calvin Martin, and we proceeded to pull the quills out. Finally when we thought we had them all out, we noticed some in the back of her mouth. This was beyond our scope, but at least we had gotten the majority of them out.

The next morning I wasted no time in calling the vet, and we took her right in. Denali had sobered up and could walk without any problem. The veterinarian didn't seem to think much of my home remedies and warned me not to administer them again without consulting them first. She did say with a large dog like Denali it probably wouldn't hurt anything but potentially could. They put Denali out, pulled the remaining quills, and $300 later she was fit as a fiddle. She shows no adverse effects to the whole incident. If drinking is bad for dogs, I doubt it is helpful for humans.

I used to think porcupines were cute. If you recall in Book 2 my brother-in-law Harlan urged me to shoot one, and I declined. However now I'm like Sandy with the puffins, I shoot every one I see. Porcupines are bad news! I even had a fellow tell me they are good eating. That's ok, I'll stick with more traditional protein sources, such as moose and bear.

Below: A drone photo of our new house. It is a little larger than our previous dwelling in Anchor Point.

Chapter 25
Paul Finds a Dead Chicken in the Van Dash

After Paul and Jo arrived in Alaska, they only had one vehicle to drive. They had driven my white van up, and then Shawn Zimmerman drove his Suburban up a week or two later. One vehicle made for some serious short-comings (I wanted my van back), so Paul asked if he could borrow Ol' Blue. That is the van that experienced a few bullet holes in an earlier book. I had been testing a theory that if a vehicle got stuck, shooting it would help get it unstuck (the theory was a fail). The upside was I now had some cool bullet holes in the side of the van. I also used this van to deliver chickens in my failed attempt at starting a chicken empire. Indeed, it had even served as a chicken coop for a short time. All this added a good deal of character to the humble vehicle. Once a stranger insulted it by telling me the van looked like something a serial killer would drive. I suspect serial killers would drive white mini vans to blend in, not rusty vans riddled with bullet holes.

After driving the van for a week Paul called and said that he had found a dead chicken embedded somewhere in the dash. This was a bit of a mystery, as normally chickens don't just crawl inside a dash and die. We calculated it may have been from the time frame the van served as a chicken coop. Equally puzzling was how a chicken could remain dead long enough to become mummified without someone smelling it. I guess we just don't drive the van enough.

Paul suggested this was a throwback to my genetics. I had a great uncle that was famous in his neighborhood for having dead cats in his kitchen. He wasn't cooking them up in soup, but perhaps rather experimenting with various embalming techniques as they were found in various states of mummification. I assured Paul that just because I had a crazy uncle, it didn't mean I was crazy. Besides, I don't think this great uncle (Wandon Diehm) ever shot holes in his vehicles. We had visitors this summer, Al and Verna Beiler, that actually knew my great uncle Wayndon, way back in the day.

It wasn't long before Paul bought an old, dumpy looking pickup. When I questioned the wisdom of him buying a vehicle when he had one he could use for free, he shrugged. He then explained that he was tired of random strangers asking him why he had bullet holes in his van. A simple stop for gas could end up taking half an hour! Paul likes to use his vehicles for evangelism, putting on big stickers like, "Are you ready for judgment?", or "Are you ready to meet God?" I told him I didn't mind if he put these stickers on the blue van, but again he declined. Some people can be hard to please. Imagine the conversation ice breakers this would provide!

Chapter 26
Shopping for Furniture

Furniture shopping is something I rarely think about, unless I wake up in a cold sweat from a nightmare caused by the idea. Once I was offered a job at a furniture store, and to this day I shudder at the very thought. True, a house should have some chairs and such, but my opinion is the less furniture the better. In fact, I laughingly told a few people that we are going to have a big empty house with no furniture. After all, we spent everything we had building the house, and then some. Might as well just enjoy it without a bunch of distractions. Marlene, however, didn't quite see eye-to-eye with me on this topic. Marlene can be glad we sold our cabin in Anchor Point around this time.

When Marlene broke the news she wanted some furniture, I pointed out that we had furniture. We brought some up from our old place in PA and also from Anchor Point. Our furniture was in a sad state of disarray. The kitchen table in Pennsylvania had been repaired with framing nails, so we left it behind. A quick note: We own a table that was given to us for a wedding gift, from my uncle Wandon Diehm's house. To the folks that gave us that--we still have it, and no, I didn't pound framing nails into that one. The heirloom table was not large enough to seat our entire family.

As I was carrying furniture into the house, Shane's dresser caught my eye. I think we had purchased it from a yard sale for $20. The faces were falling off of it. I told Marlene, "I'm not sure if I should be proud we brought this along and saved money, or if I should feel stupid for hauling this thing 4,000 miles".

My uncle works at a furniture store, and Jerry also made some custom furniture. They both said to avoid veneer products. If you're not well versed in furniture, veneer is a tiny sliver of quality looking wood glued over OSB or some kind of equally unattractive garbage. I made a mental note of this but soon discovered some downsides to non-veneer furniture.

First we looked on various classified sites for used furniture. We found a few pieces, but Marlene insisted they didn't match the paint colors. I suggested we just repaint the furniture to match, but this idea was shot down. I think we did find a few used odds and ends but nothing substantial. Next we visited some furniture stores. This proved to be mind-numbingly boring. I also discovered that non-veneer furniture is about as rare as hen's teeth. If you find any, it is also quite pricey (I did find some, but Marlene shot it down). Not what I had in mind.

The one furniture place had a bedroom set that they claimed was solid wood. It was also low priced, which made me a bit suspicious. The salesman admitted to being new at selling furniture. The combination of this

Above: I tried to talk Marlene into buying this table. It's sturdy, not veneer, and cheap! Below: The kitchen is slowly starting to look more finished. The countertops were a big plus.

Above: Wow, how tall is Jerry? Look how he fills up the doorway! Actually this is the children's built in play house, with a shorter door. Below: Our families put a hurting on the local Chinese buffet!

should have made me quick to leave the store, but being silly, I stayed and bought the bedroom set. Later I discovered that it was veneer! I felt like getting on a horse, galloping through the front doors of the store, and charging up to the customer service desk. As the horse would rear up on it's hind legs, whinnying loudly (the horse, not me), I would then point to the salesman and shout, "That bedroom set was veneer!" At this all the customers would run screaming from the store, and I would gallop out into the sunset. Sadly, I don't own any horses. Even if I did, something like that would probably be illegal, even in Alaska. Maybe Ron would loan me a draft horse.

I think we visited every furniture store on the Kenai Peninsula. Eventually we scrounged up enough furniture to meet our quota, except for the kitchen table. Every time I would ask if a table was veneer, I would get a lecture about the problems of solid wood. "The dry air makes them crack," was a common excuse. Had the veneer tables been cheap, I might have bought one anyway. But they were expensive! Who wants low quality at a high price?

The furniture industry also must think they cater to dullards. I noticed everywhere we went, there were big sales on furniture! "This must be a great time of year to buy," I thought. "Everything is on sale!" Eventually I noticed some fine print. It said, "Probably no furniture has ever been sold at the suggested retail price." Really! What good is a sale if they are just admitting that it is actually not a sale?

After exhausting ourselves and all the furniture stores in the area, we drove up to Anchorage to try some shopping. This revealed even more about the slicksters who peddle furniture. The one furniture chain had a "discount warehouse" at a separate location from their fancy store, with supposed close outs, etc. Eagerly we went to the discount warehouse to check it out. We wrote down some prices and looked at various models, but again it was all veneer. After that we went over to the regular store, which was run by the same company. The prices and furniture were the same! It was just a gimmick to trick people into thinking they were buying lower priced things. By this time I was discussing buying some plywood and making my own kitchen table. After all, in 8th grade I made a gun rack in shop class. I could handle wood! Marlene begged me to reconsider.

Of course we also went and checked out the used furniture stores in Anchorage, including the Salvation Army; But, they didn't have what we wanted. I did attempt to go into Best Buy and get something useful, but Marlene didn't think I needed a new computer or drone.

Finally, glowing like a beacon in the night, I saw a sign that said "Amish Furniture." I knew if it was Amish-made it would be good. I was a little doubtful that it was actually Amish furniture but I thought it was worth checking out.

It was actual Amish furniture! The salesman said it was made in Nappanee, Indiana. The table cost more than it would in Indiana, but by now I was beginning to not care. When I asked if the table was veneer that salesmen looked insulted. He explained this table was made from quarter sawn oak and the top was two inches think. He also assured us it would not crack from dry air. This was good enough for me. We threw the table and some matching chairs in the trailer and laid tracks back to Clam Gulch. What a miserable day of furniture shopping! Thankfully the shopping was done with good company. On the bright side I think we did eat some good hamburgers at McDonalds. I, however, was still competing in the weight loss program so I ate light.

Below: Marlene and some of our children and Jerry's children sitting at the new, Amish made table. We need some Amish up here to bring down the price of handcrafted furniture.

Chapter 27
River of Life Fellowship

The house was starting to take shape, and now that we had furniture in it we decided to start meeting there for church. As I mentioned in our last book, the plans were to start a church in the basement. This is what had caused us to forget the rancher idea and add a second story so the basement wouldn't be needed for bedrooms. Dwight had registered the non-profit organization earlier in the year, so we were set to meet. Although, I must be quick to add a church is a real church with or without paperwork.

May 28, 2017, marked the first official church service for River of Life Fellowship. Because the basement floor was still covered in mud from the drywall finishing we held the service in the living room. Present were the following families: Andy and Tabitha Stoltzfus, Dwight and Kristin Wenger, Luis and Shelley Yoder, Marv and Andi Hostetler, Jerry and Marian Martin, and of course our family. There were also a bunch of single youth guys up from Pennsylvania to help Dwight on his house. In fact they had a rather nerve-racking story, which I will relate a little later in the book.

Because we have no official preacher we took turns sharing a topic. That first Sunday Jerry volunteered to bring the topic. He had an interesting topic on heavenly treasures and rewards. He brought up the interesting point that since the streets in heaven are paved with pure gold, what possibly could be gotten of value that would be greater? He suggested our reward was seeing the souls won through our efforts on Earth. Did not Christ die for people, making their worth greater than anything else in existence? Indeed seeing people saved from Hell would be a reward. I thought Jerry had some very valid points and appreciated his sharing.

Above: Our first church meeting. There are people stacked up the steps and also behind the camera. Below: It soon become obvious we needed a larger parking area.

Chapter 28
Jerry Catches an Octopus

Jerry deserved some more fishing. Did I mention how much work he did on our house? I was so glad he and his family had come. Things would have really been rocky without their help. I don't mean that lightly! He deserved many fishing trips. My boat was in the repair shop, and I didn't really want to fork out more money for a charter. I did what I often do when I'm in a fix: I called Alan Reinford. Poor Alan, in Book 2 when I showed up and started borrowing his stuff he probably hoped I would soon just go back to Pennsylvania. Instead, here I ended up moving about a 15 minute drive from his house. Alan agreed to loan me his boat. Asking someone to borrow their boat is really nerve wracking, as it is stressful for both parties.

Speaking of boats, I should mention that I finally did the right thing, took Jesse's advice and hauled the boat to a shop. They agreed to install a new 115 HP Mercury outboard, but good things like this take time (especially in Alaska). But for various reasons the installation took a long time, two weeks longer than first expected. When you are waiting to get your boat back to go fishing that is a very long time.

Alan has a nice 20 foot aluminum boat with a newer Mercury 4 stoke. It really is very nice. June 1st, Shane, Jerry, and myself took his boat out of Homer and headed towards the fruitful waters of Port Graham. I wasn't sure where to fish, but in Alan's boat GPS was a waypoint named "Big Halibut." We figured that sounded like a good spot. It was a gorgeous day, one of the nicest I have ever seen out on the water.

Soon out of the harbor I opened up the throttle on Alan's boat. As we hit the first wave the engine faltered, then shut off. I almost panicked and figured we blew another boat motor up. Thankfully the scare was only due to a loose battery cable. We tightened it up, and off we went again.
We started fishing and at first only got a few nibbles. Then the fishing went wild! Our rods have two hooks, and soon it wasn't unusual for us to pull up two Halibut at a time. For the first time ever we started to throw halibut back (the limit is two a day). We fished and fished until we started to run low on bait. Thankfully we had caught a few pollock or cod (I'm not sure anymore) and those got chopped up for bait.

Many of the halibut we caught were small (only 5-10 pounds), and Jerry started calling them "tire kickers," and the name stuck. Now whenever we are out fishing, and we catch a small halibut or just get bites, we call them tire kickers. Although I guess if they commit by snagging a hook in their mouth they are more than just a tire kicker.

In the midst of this wild catching of fish Jerry got something big on his line. At first we were really cranked up, thinking it was a massive halibut. But this thing did not take the drag out. Instead it was like reeling up a log. When this happens I am always really curious to see what is going to turn up. We hoped it was not a rope.

Finally the thing came into sight. The first glimpse of it was a flash of orange. As it got closer we noticed a bunch of arms and legs. It was an octopus! This crazy thing had slurped up the bait and was now firmly fastened to the hook. The octopus was pretty big, and I was surprised how heavy it was. Now we also had a predicament. Is it legal to kill an octopus? How do you get it off the hook? Can they hurt you?

Jerry reached down to try and pull the hook out, and a long tentacle came up and tried to grab his arm. He shouted and pulled his hand back. The suction cups on the tentacle opened and closed menacingly. Maybe the invertebrate just wanted a hug. The octopus kept spitting water everywhere and waving all eight arms.

Finally we just cut the line. The octopus, halibut hook, and a four pound sinker sank quickly out of site. Attached to a four pound sinker, I doubt that guy will swim back up to the surface much. I'm sure he is happy hanging out at the bottom of the "pond."

While we were fishing we heard loud, bellowing roars echoing across the water. We were anchored about half a mile off shore. It sounded like a pack of grizzly bears duking it out. This perked our interest, but we could not see what was making the commotion. Later in the summer we went on a marine tour cruise out of Seward, and the mystery was solved.

Once Alan had made the comment that the Natives in Port Graham will shoot at you if you come uninvited. It is a tight-knit native community, however I doubt that it is true (later when I asked for clarification from Alan, he just laughed). I made the mistake of telling Jerry this, and he was intrigued. He wanted to go investigate this claim. Of course I am brave and all, but I didn't think today was a good day to go visit Port Graham. Instead, I suggested the wild port town of Seldovia. Both Seldovia and Port Graham are off the road system and can only be accessed by air or sea. No roads lead to them.

I assured Jerry that Seldovia was full of people that he could minister to, no need to get shot. He finally relented and with our limit of Halibut onboard we headed back. We went right by Seldovia on the way back so we swung in there and checked out the town. This was the first time I had ever been in the town. Not knowing the ropes I called Alan and asked him if it was hard to go in and dock at Seldovia. He said it was "as easy as falling off a log." So we went in and tried it. This was my first time traveling to another

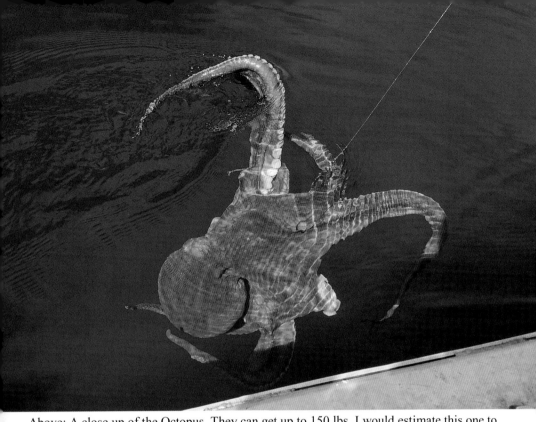

Above: A close up of the Octopus. They can get up to 150 lbs. I would estimate this one to be around 50 pounds. Below: Seldovia's harbor.

town by boat, and it felt pretty good! It made me wonder what it would be like to travel by float plane as well.

After exploring Main Street we grabbed a cup of coffee at a small cafe. The proprietor there was from Texas. He explained that he didn't like the cold, but his wife was a native Alaskan and wanted to live in Seldovia. I like Texas and all, but the climates between Alaska and Texas are quite different. We also checked out the CrabPot which is a grocery store. I inquired about renting a car, but we were told the only thing you can rent are ATVs. We did see a good many of them running up and down the streets.

We arrived back in Clam Gulch in time for supper. Before leaving that morning (or the evening before) we had agreed we would eat halibut for supper, as we had plenty in the freezer already. Upon arrival Marlene told us we had better get to filleting fish if we wanted to eat. She had decided to pin our supper plans on our fishing success! This time we got away with it; however it doesn't always work out that way!

Below: Seldovia's largest grocery store, the Crab Pot Grocery.

Chapter 29
Homeschooling in Alaska

Alaska has the best homeschool laws in the nation. All you need to do is inform the school district, if they ask, that you are homeschooling. You don't even need to bother to tell the state; you simply do not enroll your children in school anywhere. Despite this fact, there are not throngs of illiterate children roaming the streets. You would think that by the hysteria generated from homeschooling this would be the case. Remarkably all the unschooled, ignorant people I have run across up here were imported from the lower 48.

An interesting historical footnote: In 1938 one of the first things Adolf Hitler did upon becoming the dictator of Germany was outlaw homeschooling. Actually, it was five years after he became dictator, but you get the idea. Was it because he was concerned about having dull school children wandering around? In case you are wondering, he also was a fan of gun control, abortion, and genocide (I suspect he also liked raising taxes). Let's not model our lives after Adolf Hitler and the values he stood for.

In Pennsylvania (no worries, this rant is pretty short) you needed to get special permission from the local school district before homeschooling. You need to have an outline of what you are going to teach, how you are going to teach it, etc. School trips and classroom projects should be documented and turned in at the end of the year with some samples of homework. We dutifully complied and it wasn't all that difficult to comply with. In fact I took the liberty to have some fun with these reports.

Concerned that at some point the school district might tell us to stop homeschooling, I put forward a plan to demonstrate our program was superior to the state run education system. For example, in the course of one school year we were in Alaska and Florida. I compiled this as school trips in our school district report, pointing out that we wanted our children to personally investigate both hot and cold climates in the US. Over those PA homeschooling years we visited almost all the fifty states, and I dutifully included piles of photos in the portfolio. I think I might have also written up painting the limo as a home school project, explaining the value of skills in painting vehicles. I wonder if our name ever surfaced in school district meetings.

Alaska has a very generous state homeschooling program if you are interested in registering. They will pay for new computers, musical instruments, and even flight lessons! I loathe paperwork and have not signed up at this point. Shane has been asking to take flying lessons, which are not particularly cheap. Perhaps next year I will go through the bother of filling out the paperwork. And no, you don't have to teach your children about evolution if you don't want to. We teach about it, but only to point out how evolution contradicts real science and violates the laws of nature.

While living in Pennsylvania we were part of the F.A.I.T.H. home-school group. This stands for "Faith and Academics In The Home." A clever name if I say so myself. In Alaska my sister-in-law Jo started a new home school group by the same name. With 4,000 miles in between I doubt people will get the two groups mixed up.

Our first homeschool group meeting in Alaska took place on June 2 at the Kenai park. We played softball and had a carry-in. I think Paul might have also grilled hamburgers; I'm not sure. Jerry and Marian Martin also attended. I thought they fit right in up here, perhaps they will eventually trade New York for Alaska. I admire his courage for putting up with New York as long as he has, but everyone has their limit.

We are looking at doing some exciting homeschool group projects this school year. I just received a case of model rockets and a launchpad. The boys (and girls if they like) will design and build rockets and fly them. Also on the list is building and racing "rocket cars." These are powered by CO_2 bottles. My theory is that while we need some dry and boring subjects, like Math and English, the drudgery can be offset by doing interesting things.

Below: Homeschool group get together at the Kenai Park.

Chapter 30
The Six Wheeler

Sadly, Jerry and Marian's time in Alaska went quickly, and before we knew it a month was up. Marlene, Dallas, and myself ran them up to the airport. The rest of our children stayed with Marlin and Karen Eicher, or Paul and Jo. After dropping off Jerry and Marion and their family at the airport we went to Texas Roadhouse. I love steak, and steak houses are few and far between on the Peninsula. We had a great dinner there, although Dallas was frightened by the friendly aardvark guy.

As June progressed we ran into some difficult problems with our dogs. The dogs were kept about 1,000 feet from our house in the woods. We laid out an official looking "dog lot" like real Alaskan mushers with the help of Luis. Animal rights activists love to rant about Alaskan style dog lots, and they are even illegal in Pennsylvania (what isn't). The dogs are tethered to a six or seven foot chain, which is attached to a post. Activists will say how terrible it is that the dogs can only move six or seven feet.

But the truth of the matter is that it is more like twelve or fourteen feet. Not only that, the dogs run in circles around the post and get all the exercise they want. Furthermore, the dogs are harnessed up and exercised regularly. Ironically activists also take issue with this, saying the dogs are forced to work. How cruel! Actually the dogs are not forced to run or work. If a dog does not want to run; you can't make it run. End of story. Sure, a fat English Bulldog that sits in an apartment on a couch all day might not want to go out and run ten miles. But dogs such as Siberian Huskies or any variation of them love to run. I am opposed to people being cruel to dogs, but I don't think feeding dogs their favorite food (fish and high energy kibble) and having them do their favorite thing (run) is being cruel at all. Many activist organizations, including the HSUS, make ending pet ownership part of their end goal. Just read the fine print on their website. The more extreme variants (PETA) say that pigs, rats, and boys are all the same. According to their logic, if you have more rodents in your house than people, the proper thing to do would be to throw the people out of the house. Is this really the product of a sane mind? Another case in point: They label the folks at Kentucky Fried Chicken as serial killers.

Anyway, all this to say that the dogs were kept a good distance from the house. This was because our yard around the house was not very big; it turned into muskeg quickly. The only option was to keep them a good distance from the house. This was fine and worked well until the swamp (aka muskeg) started to break down from driving four wheelers through it every day. The problems started out small at first. Shane (his job was to feed the dogs) would come walking in and say that the one four wheeler

Left: Poor Dallas was terrified of Andy the Aardvark, the mascot for Texas Roadhouse. We only had Dallas along to drop Jerry and Marian's family off, so we took advantage of this to grab a quiet meal at a "fancy" restaurant.

Below: I saw this Mallard for sale beside the road. It made me so happy it wasn't mine I stopped and took a picture of it. Not to my surprise, it had a For Sale sign on it! This was not the same hide-

was stuck. I would run out with the one not stuck and winch him out. This started happening every day. Then one tragic day we got both four wheelers stuck deep in the mud. Nothing was going anywhere. Because we hauled all the water out (we didn't want to feed the dogs swamp water) and thirty pounds or more of food a day it was difficult carrying it by hand. Muskeg is very tiring to walk through without hauling a bunch of extra weight. It is very spongy and saps your energy.

Marlene and I discussed our options. We could build a nice new gravel lane through the swamp, making travel back and forth easy. I priced this with some excavators. The price tag: $50,000. Ouch. That was certainly a no go. It would be cheaper just to buy non swamp land somewhere to put the dogs. Then I remembered a faint memory from childhood. I was at my uncle Abe's place (the fellow that makes the handmade muzzleloaders), and he had a vehicle that looked like a bathtub with six wheels on it. It would float and could be used on land or water. Something like that could be a cheap ticket to solving our problem!

I was not sure what this vehicle was called, so I did some research. There were several companies that made vehicles like this. The most common design was called an Argo and came in six and eight wheel configurations. It turned out the largest Argo dealer in the world was located in Anchorage, only a three hour drive from the house. Naturally I also checked out some used Argo's on Craigslist. The problem with Argos are that they are more complex in nature than a regular four wheeler. Once they are worn they can be very problematic and cause an ongoing "nickel and dime" situation. I'm ok with having old cheap vehicles where parts are easily obtained and road service is covered by insurance, but having an ATV that breaks down is inexcusable.

I have learned that it is best to run ideas past Marlene before implementing them. Most ideas that skip this step end up in outright disaster. Marlene said she was tired of us "fooling around in the swamp" and given the lack of alternatives said to go for it. She did suggest we buy the base model and not one with a diesel engine for $40,000.

In mid-June sometime we hitched up the trailer and headed for Anchorage. I was glad to be shopping for something worthwhile this time around. We arrived at the dealership and checked out the inventory. There were some real nifty models to be had, for sure. Some of them even came with cabs and heaters! Those obviously were used by the oil companies, as nobody else could afford those models. The high end Argos cost as much as a new pickup! Naturally we steered towards the bottom end of the spectrum, and ended up looking at the no frills six wheeler.

There was a Search and Rescue model six wheeler for an extra $3,000. It was painted camouflage and had some nifty lights and a brush guard. I was drawn to it like a magnet. Thankfully Marlene brought me back to my senses. For three grand I can paint a lot of things camouflage! The search and rescue model did come with a winch installed already.

I tried to haggle on price. Stifling a chuckle, the dealer insisted the prices he gave us were the lowest he could go. Never take a trailer and eager children along when you go ATV shopping. It is best to first grow a beard, then take your oldest, ugliest vehicle (I should have driven 'Ol Blue). Then you talk real slow and stroke your beard for about fifteen minutes. The salesman will grow nervous thinking that you are a well-rounded, mature individual carefully weighing all the pros and cons of his sale offering. Fearing he will be exposed as the highest priced guy on the planet, the sales person will blurt out lower and lower prices until you finally sign the sales contract. This approach has never worked for me, mostly because I can't stand having a beard. Josh claims his beard balm would help.

For an ATV to be actually useful in Alaska it must have a winch. Originally I planned to get a winch from Harbor Freight and install it myself. However the dealer was running a promotion and said I could get $1,500 off accessories. If I got no accessories, I got no promotion. Installed, the Warn winch package was a mind blowing $1,800. This seemed ridiculously overpriced, but with the $1,500 instant rebate it brought it down to an extra $300. I decided it was worth $300 to add a winch, also this price was installed. If I installed it myself, the thing would probably let loose at a critical moment and take someone's head off.

Towing the Argo back was easy. I was concerned it would weigh a lot but the actual weight was only a bit more than the Kymco four wheeler. It was interesting noting how many people stopped and stared at the Argo. They cost only slightly more than a four wheeler, but I guess are not as well known.

Indeed the Argo did blast through mud and muskeg! We pulled the four wheelers out in short order. This episode also inadvertently started a rather hilarious rumor: That I had so much money when my four wheelers got stuck I just got a new one instead of pulling them out. This also proves that rumor wrong; I did pull the four wheelers out and didn't leave them to rust to pieces. As far as the money part, that is easy. Just buy some old vehicles and roll the savings over into more useful areas of life. Skip that new mini van, and just go buy an old rusty limo.

And really, anyone can afford an Argo. Think about this scenario: You are sitting in a doctor's office, across from a sober faced physician. He tells you that you have a terminal disease with only one known cure. Your mind races, and you wonder how much this treatment will cost. Will it be $100,000? Or a million dollars? Ten million? Deliberately he throws an Argo

Above: The Argo loaded on our dilapidated old trailer that we hauled up from Pennsylvania.
Below: Shane and Desiree take the Argo for a spin around our bleak grassless yard.

Above: The view from the Argo while it is floating in the pond. Below: Paul takes the Argo on a spin through our pond, located behind the house.

sales brochure in front of you. He says, "Your only hope is to buy one of these." That sounds like a pretty affordable cure, doesn't it? Now let's put that rumor to pasture that only wealthy people can afford Argos.

Marlene had some serious reservations about driving the newly purchased, fresh from the factory Argo through a pond. She made the mistake of watching people sink their Argos on YouTube. It does seem to be a common problem. I assured her I was above such foolishness and could safely float the Argo. To err on the side of caution I invited Paul Weaver over to help. We discovered right away that you can get a six wheeler stuck. The pond bank was really muddy, and we got stuck before even entering the water. I suspected something like this might happen, so I stepped out of the vehicle. Immediately I was up to my chest in mud! I could hardly move! Now, I did have the presence of mind to wear chest waders.

Eventually I was able to work my way out of the mud and walk back to the house. By the time I arrived back with the four wheeler Paul had managed to get the Argo into the pond. He was driving in circles, the tires kicking up muddy water everywhere. He certainly seemed to be enjoying himself. After Paul saw I returned he attempted to drive back out of the pond but got stuck. I quickly winched him right out with the four wheeler. We made several more runs in and out of the pond. The Argo was quite tipsy. I don't think I want to try taking it out in a lake. Perhaps the eight wheeler models are more stable. It certainly did float though! And I had to laugh when I looked at the registration information. It appears you can decide to register it as a boat or an ATV. Talk about options! I wonder if it is legal to drive a registered boat down a public four wheeler trail?

Below: Winching the Argo out of the pond. These things certainly float! Just don't forget the plug...

Chapter 31
An Alligator Head Comes in the Mail

As you may remember, in our Nome book we shot some alligators in Florida. Shooting alligators may seem a little contradictory in a book about Nome, Alaska, but let's not be all closed minded and such. We had dropped those gators off at a taxidermist in Florida and ordered a mounted head for Shane. They were going to mail it up to our place in Alaska when it was finished. Shane asked me nearly every day, "Do you think my alligator head will come today?" I assured him lots of boys his age have to wait for alligator heads in the mail, and he was no exception. He needed to learn patience.

One day, the taxidermist shop called and told me they mailed the alligator head. I didn't tell Shane, as I figured it could just be a surprise. He was excited and delighted when the head finally made its appearance. Now he has it proudly hanging on his wall. I did wish a tiny bit that I could still submit school work portfolios to the Pennsylvania school district. No doubt I would label that entry as biology class.

Chapter 32
First Visitors of 2017

We have had a flood of visitors stopping in the past year who read our books, which is very humbling and amazing. We are honored when people want to stop in and visit. Unfortunately, I can't list everyone who stopped in, because I simply don't remember everyone. We'll have to get a guest book, and maybe I will include excerpts from that in future books.

A tip for getting into my future books: The more memorable you are the better. One visitor removed his leg in the living room. That certainly works! Or, paint your vehicle camouflage with spray cans from Walmart. That is sure to get a mention! It is also good if you give us a little bit of a heads up; email works best. Just email me at thesnaders@gmail.com. One family did email us, but stopped in before I responded. That was fine, but we had been up all night, and there were remains of 70 salmon scattered all over the kitchen. There is also the risk we will be out gold panning (or doing local charitable works in the community) and not at home. The best sure fire way to see us is simply come visit our church on a Sunday morning.

Email me for directions, as we don't always have church at the same address, and as time progresses we may find a permanent spot for it.

The first visitors were Michael and Mary Lois Petersheim, along with their children, Jeffrey, Abigail, Joanna, Nathaniel, and Catherine. Michael's parents, Sam and Sarah, were also along. What caught my attention with Michael was his traveling vehicle. Anyone can go out, buy a motorhome, and drive it around. But that approach is really somewhat boring. Instead Michael bought a 1991 Ford Shuttlebus and renovated it by combining it with an old pull behind camper he found on craigslist (or somewhere similar). They also pulled a rather vintage looking camper behind the bus.

On the Alcan highway near the Alaskan border there is a series of rather enormous frost heaves. Come to think about it, there are frost heaves all over the Alcan highway. As they traveled over these frost heaves they noticed the vintage looking camper growing longer. It appeared the frame was beginning to come apart, as the gaps in the door and other places seemed to keep expanding. Finally they found a hardware store somewhere along the route and managed to patch it back together.

That particular Sunday we had decided to meet at the park in Soldotna. I was in charge, and I don't remember exactly what I talked about. I think it may have been the faith chapter in Hebrews. Anyway, Michael and his family were there, and we had a good time chatting and playing the game where you figure out who you know that knows each other. Michael's church was part of the Keystone Conference, which Crossroads Mennonite Church is a part of. There were quite a few connections through this. It is usually a small world.

Below: Michael and Mary Lois Petersheim family, along with Michael's parents Sam and Sarah Petersheim. They are in front of the improvised Ford Bus. Not a bad rig but it could use some camouflage paint.

Chapter 33
Fishing With the New Boat Motor

After what seemed like years, but couldn't have been more than a few months, I got my boat back with a shiny new 115 HP four stroke Mercury outboard. Being my cool, collected self I decided that I should try the new motor out as soon as possible, in the off event there were some warranty or installation issues to address with the mechanic. The motor, to my shock, had cost more than the original quote. But by using careful math I figured that I could recoup that lost amount by taking an additional ten fishing trips that summer on top of what I already planned. This would lower the average cost per trip so that it would now fit in my original budget. Sometime I may write a book on financial planning, and even consider calling in to the Dave Ramsey financial consulting show. That Dave guy tends to get all technical though, so I was worried he would just start yelling about some irrelevant detail I overlooked. Once Paul said he heard him tell a caller that he shouldn't visit Alaska to go fishing! I don't support crazy talk like that.

Finally, (after about 20 seconds), I talked Paul into going fishing with me. We decided we would go back to the spot Jerry, Shane, and I went. This time we would not limit out at six fish. By putting as many children in the boat as possible and staying out over midnight, we could legally bring back many more halibut. Gleefully we calculated our bag limit. With seven people in the boat we could catch fourteen fish before midnight and fourteen fish after midnight, for a grand total of 28 halibut! That fruitful day with Jerry we threw probably twenty halibut back. This was going to be fun!

Around five or six in the evening we left my house and headed towards Homer. Emotions were running high, after all, we had a new boat motor, four halibut rods, and lots of bait. The trip was dampened a little by all the children climbing over everything, but a little fishing is necessary for a well-rounded education.

After launching the boat, we headed down to fish off the coast of Seldovia. This is where we had the windfall of halibut and sharks with Henry Swarey the year before. Oddly, the fishing proved to be poor at this spot. We decided we must press on towards that "Big Halibut" spot which had been programmed into Alan's GPS. Of course I took the liberty of copying the coordinates over to my own GPS (I'm sure Alan wouldn't have minded).

As we cruised along doing about 34 mph I heard Paul give a shout. He was motioning and trying to communicate something. Slowing the boat down so I could hear, Paul demonstrated with hand motions that he just saw our kicker motor fly off the back and disappear into the wake. What a bad deal! If a kicker motor flies off into the inlet, that is pretty much the end of it.

If anyone reading this book happens to find it, you can keep it with a clear conscience.

Soon we reached Port Graham. It was now about 11 P.M., and we still had not caught any fish. We needed to start bringing them in fast if we wanted to catch fourteen by midnight. Furiously we fished and fished, but no success! It was here that I started to learn an interesting lesson about fishing, and that is the fish don't always bite! Maybe I'm the only one who has experienced this phenomenon. Around 20 minutes till midnight Shane got his line stuck on something on the bottom. He wanted to cut his line and let $15 worth of tackle go to the bottom. I disapproved of this and asked Paul to try and work the line while I drove in circles with the boat. Sometimes if you circle around a hook or sinker that is stuck in a rock it will pull loose, because you are pulling on it from a different angle.

After about five minutes of working this loose, we had almost decided to just cut the line. Suddenly the line started jerking, and it went off in another direction! Now there was a fish on it! Three times we had the fish near the boat, and three times it headed down again. We were fishing in about 100 feet of water, so it took some time to work the fish back up. I was excited. I knew that a fish acting this way was pretty big and not just a tire kicker.

Finally, Paul got the beast into the boat. It was way too big for the net, and I would have considered shooting it in the head, but by some oversight the only gun in the boat was a .454 Casull, not really something you want to use to shoot objects in the water from three feet away. I took the gaff out and slammed it into the fish, only to have it bounce off! To my horror the fish dived again, but not very far, only maybe ten feet. Paul quickly worked it back up, and I again hit it with the gaff, finally making it stick. I could tell the fish was heavy as we hauled it onboard.

A fish this big can really damage people and things in the boat if not dispatched quickly. I was fairly pumped up with adrenaline, so I sat on it and beat it over the head with the fish whacker for awhile. To my dismay, Makayla was taking a video of the whole spectacle. I must say I did not look dignified in it. When the kicker motor up and left, it had disconnected from the fuel line, causing gasoline to spill all over the rear of the boat (the line was quickly plugged after we realized what happened). We didn't want to ruin the tasty, mild flavored halibut with gasoline so we perched the giant fish up in the front beside some of the children. There was no way it would fit into the boat's live well!

Paul had hauled in the big fish just before midnight. I told him he might as well catch two more! But despite our efforts we caught no more fish. Thankfully the big fish we caught made us feel happy despite only having one. Soon after midnight we pulled the plug on the trip and headed back towards Homer. The sun didn't really set on that fishing trip, although it did dip below the horizon. We could see the entire time without flashlights.

It was nearing four in the morning when we pulled into our house in Clam Gulch. Now I was glad we didn't have 28 halibut onboard! We rolled some paper out on the garage floor to butcher the one and only halibut we brought back. First however, we weighed it. It weighed 64 pounds! Not bad, although someday I plan to catch a larger one. Just the other summer some-one brought a 400 lb. halibut back to Ninilchik. Anything over 150 pounds is a bit of a rarity in this area, so don't expect 400 pounders every trip.
Paul did the honors of filleting the fish, and I vacuumed packed it and got it ready for the freezer. Jo and the remaining Weaver children had slept in the camper so after packing up the fish we all went to bed. Around ten in the morning we got up, ate breakfast, and then Paul and Jo headed for their home in Sterling.

Below: Paul proudly displays a fish from Pennsylvania. It might even be a state record, who knows. I prefer Alaskan fishing.

Paul's Alaskan fish, a 64 pound Halibut

Chapter 34
Andrew Stoltzfus Wins a Suburban

Andy and Tabitha moved to twenty acres they had purchased the year before in Anchor Point. Their land was only about two miles from my place that I sold. I felt a little bad leaving the neighborhood after they moved in. But we still lived close to them by Alaska standards, being only 35 miles up the road. I also had 40 acres close to them that I hoped to build another cabin on at some point.

Readers may recall an off roading expedition in the Suburban in Book 3, in which I got it firmly stuck in the muskeg. My four wheeler had broken down and it was moose season. I tried using the Suburban in place of a four wheeler but that approach failed. Thankfully it had gotten stuck on the forty acres that I had not sold, otherwise it would be locked into the annals of history. After it sat there two years I began to realize that I might not ever get it out. It was a bit of an eyesore, although not worse than many other properties in Anchor Point. Being a generous person, I told Andy that if he was able to remove the Suburban from the swamp, I would give it to him as a reward!

Andy knew a good deal when he saw one. A few days later he sent me a text asking what to do if a bulldozer was stuck in muskeg. My heart fell, and I could imagine us fruitlessly pushing on a 20 ton piece of equipment. I could see in the future that Alan Reinford's D8 Cat would be there, rusting beside the Suburban. A thousand years from now archaeologists would be promoting theories of why some guy parked a suburban and a bulldozer beside each other in a swamp. They would likely come up with all kinds of fancy theories involving religious ceremonies or social order, but it would probably never occur to them the vehicles just got stuck there. Who knows, maybe it would even end up in some chart about evolution.

Thankfully, Andy did not get the bulldozer stuck. He had only sent me the text message hoping I would think it had gotten stuck. Andy was able to carefully push his new Suburban out of the swamp with the dozer. Later, in an elaborate ceremony with much fanfare I awarded Andy the much coveted Suburban title. He did his best to appear unemotional.

Above: Andrew Stoltzfus is thrilled to receive the title to the 1986 Chevy Suburban. Hopefully I don't look too gaunt, as this is right at the tail end of the weight loss contest.
Below: I also traded Andrew my old Rabbit, and he proceeded to smash it up with a skid loader! I think he wanted to use the diesel engine to power a generator.

Chapter 35
Fishing With an Airplane Mechanic

Dwight Wenger is an airplane mechanic and works at Mission Aviation Repair Center in Soldotna, AK. He is also working on building a house, which fills up a good deal of his spare time. His father-in-law, Howard, came up to help on the building project. Because I like to provide encouragement to missionaries, I told Dwight I could take him fishing. So we planned an evening outing with Dwight and his father-in-law.

As we loaded the boat with gear and tackle, I noticed Dwight checking out the one trailer tire. "This tire looks shot," he commented. I chuckled, and assured Dwight it was nothing to worry about, telling him how many times I made the trip to Homer and back on this "lame" tire. Dwight didn't seem convinced. He also brought up the fact I had no kicker motor (it had flown off into the inlet in a previous fishing trip). "I have a new outboard engine," I pointed out. "Nothing could go wrong." Again my reassurances didn't seem to inspire confidence.

As I was unloading at the dock at Homer, Dwight again seemed to question the boat's seaworthiness. "Does this thing have a bilge pump?" he asked. I smiled and pointed down to the small pump located at the back of the boat. "Yup, right there," I answered. This didn't seem to satisfy him. "But there is just a pump, there is no hose connected to it." I looked closer. Sure enough, the pump was just sitting there, with no hose anywhere to be seen. I turned the pump on. It simply made little ripples in the water around it. I had always wondered why it didn't work, and that explained it. "Don't worry," I assured Dwight. "If it leaks too much we'll figure a way to get the water out." I decided we needed to leave soon before Dwight lost interest in fishing. He clearly was not used to improvising.

Perhaps we should have just left the boat in the dock, as the fish did not bite that evening. We were fishing the clam tides which is usually a bad idea (Clam tides are really large tides, as high as 20 feet). But this was the only evening that would work, so we took it. Howard claimed he never caught fish, so I decided to go the entire way down to Port Graham, to the spot Paul caught the 64 pound halibut. Something like that would certainly cheer Howard up. But we fished all night, well half the night, without any fish.

When we returned in the dark of night Dwight and Howard both seemed dismayed when I reported the trailer lights didn't work. I explained that trailer lights in the Alaskan summer really are a waste of money, it hardly ever gets dark. Sure, it was dark now, but in an hour or two the sun would come up (I like to plan ahead).

Several times I took Dwight and Howard fishing. Once Dwight's brother-in-law Luke, and his grandfather also went along. The only fish we caught were miserable Irish Lords. These fish are not any good to eat. Howard claims it is impossible for him to catch fish-but I am sure it is not. I hope he returns in 2018, and this time: We will catch fish.

Chapter 36
Weight Loss Results

July 3rd was the big day when everyone weighed in. Towards the end of May I had so much going on, that I almost forgot about the weight loss contest. It was like a dim memory in the back of my mind, when one day I remembered it. I thought, "Oh, no, I blew this one!" However when I weighed myself I had lost five or six pounds that week without trying. Stress and hauling heavy things around constantly must do that to a person. Anyway, I decided that it was no time to quit, and started paying close attention to it again.

As much as I like to consider myself a serious weight-loss athlete, there is another fellow that is in a league above me. I don't remember his name, and I'm sure he is humble enough he wouldn't want me to throw it around anyway. This guy won not only one weight loss contest, but the same contest twice! He won at least one trip to Alaska (my kind of guy). It takes some serious discipline to put on enough weight to do that. Rumor has it that part of his discipline regimen was waking up in the middle of the night, frying some eggs, then going back to bed. While training up to a weight loss championship the key is maximizing calories while minimizing exercise. Of course, the downside is that for the losing weight part of the cycle you then need to reverse this strategy. Some people find this troublesome and simply skip this step and just start weight training all over again.

In this weight loss contest I was a part of, the winner received $1,800. Second and third place got nothing, along with the rest of the pack. Being in Alaska gave me a slight advantage, as I had four extra hours to lose weight because of the time zone variation. This did bother my conscience, so I would occasionally eat some ice cream to make up the difference. The last three or four days I made a mad dash to the finish line and didn't eat anything. The final weigh in results?

Sadly, out of a pack of 18 contenders I only placed fourth, losing a total of 36.2 pounds. The winner lost 37.9 pounds. Now had I lost two more pounds I still wouldn't have placed first, because they were going by percentage of weight lost compared to starting body weight. But a few additional pounds would have done it! I could have kicked myself for not skipping a few more hamburgers. Imagine all the fast food, candy, and soda pop I could have bought with $1,800! On a side note, my brother-in-law Mike didn't even come close to winning. This was due to him not having enough raw material to work with at the beginning of the contest. Training pays off!

Chapter 37
A Visitor's Leg Falls Off

One group of visitors who stopped in this summer was David and Cindy Martin from Lebanon, Pennsylvania. Their children Andrea, Rochelle, Weston, Larson, and Tristan were along. I wish they would have brought some Lebanon sweet bologna with them, as it is hard to come by up here. Fred Meyer's sells it for almost the same price as Halibut! They had a fishing trip planned and had stopped in on their way to Ninilchik.

David works at a feed mill (I think he might own it, not sure) and had the unfortunate experience of getting his foot caught in an auger. The whole ordeal sounded rather unpleasant. Let's just say there is no really good way to chop up your foot. Since this whole incident only happened last year, David had spent quite a bit of time the past winter reading, and I must say he is a very discerning reader. Some of the books he mentioned were of utmost quality.

Rochelle told me that they use LancasterPuppies.com to advertise their puppies. This got my hearty approval. Then she made a comment that, "it works so good they don't use anything else anymore." Now we're talking! They use our self list feature to upload their own pictures.

I have always been curious what a fake leg looks like up close, but this isn't something you really go around pursuing. It would be a little awkward to approach someone and ask if they had a fake leg, and that you would like a closer look if they did. Once I told my brother Andrew that my aunt Alma had a fake nose. She was in the next room, and he wasn't shy at all about going and looking, prompting her to ask, "Andrew! What are you looking at!" He was much younger at the time.

Unlike what I imagine many people with fake limbs to be like, David was not shy at all. He popped the leg off right in the middle of the living room. Dallas seemed stunned by these developments and stood staring at the leg for a long time. He even tried on the rubber foot! It is amazing what they can do with prosthetic limbs these days, as David doesn't even walk with a limp. This could make for some interesting tricks to play on people. For example you could shoot your foot when hunting with strangers, and they would all panic. If you do try that, make sure you get the correct foot, and that you're not standing in a boat. Or perhaps you could squirrel away a survival kit in the leg. I have heard of people smuggling Bibles that way. The only problem with that plan is you would have few qualifying volunteers, unless they were extremely committed to the cause.

David and his family didn't catch any fish on their first round with Ninilchik Saltwater Charters because the weather forced them in almost as soon as they got out on the inlet. But they did get a second go of it a few days later and landed some really nice fish!

Above: Dallas seems stumped by the removable leg.

Right: Dallas warms up to the removable leg and even tries on the rubber foot. It is a bit large for him.

Chapter 38
Richard Builds a Free Deck

We have some friends, Richard and Karen Stauffer, who had been talking about visiting for quite some time. Richard is not the type of guy who likes to just sit around, so we made a deal where I would fly them up if he would build us a deck. Sound familiar? Richard and his family landed in Anchorage on July 4th.

On the way to the airport we stopped at a Wendy's to get some food. Oh, the delicious glory! I felt like dumping my cup of Dr. Pepper on the floor and rolling in it. And the French fries! Talk about exquisite. I'm not sure what that particular restaurant did differently than the others in that chain or even the whole area, but the food was delicious.

At the airport we had a bit of a difficult time finding Richard, Karen, and their family. I was walking around with my cell phone talking to Richard. Both of us were confused as to where the other one was. Suddenly I bumped into someone, and I turned around. Here Richard and I were standing back to back trying to figure out where the other one was! We loaded them and their family into the van, and we headed south to Clam Gulch. It was tough, fitting both our families and luggage into the van. Maybe I'll have to look for a larger four wheel drive vehicle.

Richard didn't waste any time starting on the deck. First we had Dan Zimmerman come out and dig a line for the outdoor furnace to connect to the house. He also dug in some sono tubes for a deck footer. Later that day, we went to Home Depot to pick out some lumber for the deck. It takes a substantial amount of lumber, and we had brought my little trailer along. I was doubtful it was big enough. After looking around and finding out almost everything we needed was not in stock, we gave up and decided to just call Spenard Builders Supply. This turned out to be a much more efficient choice. We called in the order ahead of time and then borrowed Marlin's flatbed trailer (the same one he bought from me in Book 3), and the Spenard guys just set the pulled and banded stack of lumber on with a forklift. That sure beats pushing little metal carts overflowing with heavy lumber around Home Depot.

The next day we sneaked a quick fishing trip in. The concrete was coming sometime in the early afternoon so we got up at 5 A.M. and headed down to Homer. We cruised on over to Anchor Point and fished the approximate location that David Martin said they had fished. There were some trench-like structures that looked promising on the map, and we wanted to hit these. Halibut tend to be bottom feeders (although not always, as evidenced by Shane's 60 pound fish), and they like to hang out around cliffs and changes in underwater terrain.

Above: Richard makes sure the sono tube is installed at the correct location. Below: Spenards just set the bundle of lumber right on the trailer. Do you recognize this trailer from anywhere? It shows up in a previous book. It now belongs to Marlin Eicher.

At first the fishing was slow, but then we started getting nibbles. Unfortunately we had a time schedule to keep and just before we had to leave, we started really pulling in Halibut. With three or four onboard we hightailed it back to the Homer dock, and we managed to beat the concrete truck. We almost didn't make it, because we had a tire explode on the boat trailer, and it took a few minutes to change it. I was glad we made it back, because Dan Zimmerman, who was there doing some more excavating, told us that if the truck showed up, and we weren't there, he wasn't pouring it!

Paul told us of a wild fishing trip he had taken with Marlin that week. He spoke of a secret bay, tucked back in the mountains that was flooded with rivers of salmon. This sounded very interesting, and Paul promised to ride out with Richard, Shane, and myself. Paul assured us we would catch salmon here like never before. This wasn't hard for me to beat, as with the exception of dipnetting, I had never caught more than one or two salmon in my entire life.

Below: Shane fillets our catch from the morning. It's a shame we had to leave when we did, I'm sure we could have caught more. They were biting briskly when we left.

Above: I have never seen someone work as fast as Richard. Well, maybe my cousin Adam would come close. Below: The deck, almost finished.

Chapter 39
Marine Tour

Marlene, Dallas, and I went along with Richard's family on a marine tour out of Seward. There are several tour companies that will take you by boat to see glaciers, whales, and all sorts of marine life in the Kenai Fjords National Park. These cruises are a bit pricey but might be worth it. To save money Richard and I just thought about following the tour boat in our little boat. Ships are required by law to assist other boats in distress so it would have been insurance in case we ran into boat problems. However, we decided this might be a bad idea. The cruise we took covered 110 miles and lasted for eight hours.

We intentionally had been watching the weather and, seeing a nice day, quickly booked a tour. This is yet another reason to come and stay awhile. If you plan everything to the minute ahead of time, you will probably be doing half of your activities in the rain. Plus the best way to ruin a good vacation is to try and plan everything down to the minute. You might as well just go do your taxes and start an accounting business; it would be the same level of fun.

Only about a mile out of the harbor, we started seeing whales. In addition, we got to see some walruses. This solved one of the mysteries from the earlier fishing trip with Jerry off Port Graham. Walruses growl and roar like enraged grizzly bears and was undoubtedly the sound we heard while fishing. I have read that a walrus can kill a polar bear that is in the water. This sounded interesting, but we didn't see any polar bears that day.

Marine tours have their downside. I don't particularly enjoy throngs of people. On a marine tour boat you need to just pick a spot on the deck and hold your position, hoping you might see some wildlife and not get pushed overboard. How it typically works on one of these boats is this: Someone will shout, "Whale off to port!" And everyone in the boat stampedes like heifers over to that corner. Unless you are grossly overweight and very rude, you will have no chance at seeing anything of this alleged whale. If by chance a whale is spotted that is best viewed from where you are, you had best snap a few good pictures then hang on as the herd rushes up. We saw several killer whales that day. I suspect they hang out in the cruise ship areas hoping to snack on the poor souls shoved overboard in the stampedes.

Watching the glaciers calve was a really neat experience. It sounds like thunder as huge chunks of ice fall off into the sea. The masses of ice themselves would creak and groan. The staff on the boat pulled up a chunk of ice and served drinks with it. It was a couple dollars a glass so we just let it slide. Glacier ice fizzes when it dissolves, I think this is due to the atmosphere changes when the ice was frozen years ago compared to the current atmospheric pressure.

Above: Yours truly and his beautiful wife on the Marine Tour boat in front of the calving glacier.

Right: Orcas swimming past the boat. Don't be fooled by the picture, these whales can get to be 28 feet long and weigh several tons.

Chapter 40
Rivers of Salmon

Friday of that same week we again headed out, this time with Paul Weaver onboard. The problem with this secret bay was you could only access it at high tide. If you weren't paying attention you would get stuck in there and have to wait until the tide came back up. The tide usually takes around 12 hours to cycle. No roads lead to this little bay, so you are really stuck if the tide keeps you in. Because of small things like this, I always keep an emergency kit with matches, hatchet, etc, in the boat.

After some boating in circles we located the bay. This little bay is not really much of a secret, but I would hate to have it flooded out with fishermen, so I won't print the name of it. However, if you stop in at my place in Clam Gulch I will let you in on the secret. It took us awhile to navigate the small stream that connected the cove, and we got hung up a few times. But because the tide was coming up all we needed to do was wait a little bit. It was loaded with fish, that's for sure. Salmon jumped everywhere, as far as the eye could see.

In this cove you could snag. This procedure is simple. All you need to do is attach a large weighted treble hook to your line and cast out and briskly reel in. It usually doesn't take long, and you have a salmon on the line! Some folks argue this is a poor excuse for fishing, and you should get the fish to bite your hook. If that's how you think, good for you. You're welcome to go fish somewhere else in a different boat. Now pay attention though: Snagging is only legal in certain parts of Cook Inlet. Do not just snag anywhere you feel like it.

We started hauling in salmon left and right. Snagging is hard on your hook and line and we started losing hooks. To our great dismay we had only two or three extra hooks in the whole boat! There was a bag of extra hooks somewhere but not in our boat. Before long we were down to one hook. A few fish were still needed to max out our limits, and we were trying to snag with old lures, halibut hooks, and anything we could find in the boat.

Suddenly, like a beacon of light in the night, Gareth cruised up in Alan's boat. They had just arrived to get in on the fun. Desperately I asked Gareth if he had extra hooks along. With a quick grin, he pitched several over into our boat, and we were back in business! Several other Sterling Mennonite Church guys were with Gareth. In fact, they had brought two boats. With the extra hooks we had our limit in a few minutes. Many of the salmon were pinks, but a good bit were reds too (reds are generally considered more desirable). This was early in the season, and all the fish were fresh off the salt water so we just kept everything we caught. Catch and release snagging is really not the best idea in the world, but the salmon in the cove are all going to die anyway.

Above: Paul and Ma-
kayla fishing.

Fish everywhere! Neither Richard or I
enjoy fishing in the lower 48, but we
are hooked on it in Alaska. Paul enjoys
fishing anytime, anywhere, even for
rodent sized fish.

After catching our limit of salmon we headed back to the dock. From this bay it takes about 45 minutes to reach Homer. As we were loading up the boat to return home Richard wondered if we could come back fishing tomorrow. I replied I couldn't think of any good reason not to, and so our plans for Saturday were set!

Shane with a salmon. I think this one is a red. The only way I can tell for sure is cutting a hunk out of the side to see the color of the meat. This is discouraged for catch and release fishing.

Above: We had to share the bay with crowds of other boats.

Below: Not a bad haul for an hour of fishing (or less).

Chapter 41
Fire in the Boat!

Saturday morning we headed down to Homer once again. On the way down I texted Gareth to see what their results were from the evening before. Here they were still at the dock filleting fish! They had quite the haul from the night before. By fishing past midnight they had managed to double their legal limit. They had over 32 halibut and some ridiculously huge amount of salmon. They threw everything back but the reds, or they would have had a small mountain of fillets.

Remembering the free hooks from the evening before I offered to get Gareth and his crew some coffee at McDonalds. He must have been tired, because he took me up on it (Gareth is not a fan of the golden arches).

We stopped at the Ulmer's Hardware Store for something, probably snagging hooks, before stopping by McDonalds. There we noticed a lady get in a vehicle with a Mennonite style head covering. In Lancaster or Holmes County, this is a very common thing to see. Not so much in Homer, Alaska. I told Richard we should wait and see who it was when they drove past. Here it was Marlin Swarey and his family. You may remember Marlin from the ill-fated attempt at launching a boat off Whisky Gulch beach in Book 3, *The Year of Much Fishing*. This was the incident where we tried to go fishing early in the day and ended up finally launching at ten in the evening.

Marlin Swarey pulled up beside us and wondered what we were up to. Here my selfish side kicked in. "I hope he doesn't want to go along fishing," I thought. Please understand, this wasn't because I didn't like Marlin. That day we had hoped to travel pretty far in the boat. My boat is fairly small and every extra person affects the handling. Legally I can haul six people or 850 pounds in the boat. Plus, the boat is a bit cramped, and every extra person makes things more complicated. That day we had hoped to head about ten miles out to a spot Marlin Eicher recommended for halibut, and then head on over to the salmon bay.

I asked Marlin why he was in Homer, as they normally live near Palmer which is about a six hour drive away. They serve at Victory Bible Camp, coincidentally the same camp that my grandma had helped at 25 or 30 years ago. He said they were in Homer for a missionary conference or something. I don't remember quite what or why. Anyway, they had booked a halibut charter for that day. When they showed up at the charter office they were told someone made a mistake, and there was no room. They were given a refund and a free hat. What a deal! I can think of better ways to get free hats. In the middle of July it is nearly impossible to get an unscheduled seat on a charter, short of just stealing a boat.

With that kind of sad story, I wasn't about to turn Marlin away. We only had three people in the boat; there was plenty of room for one more. Marlin commented that his sister-in-law also wanted to come along, so we made room for her too. They agreed to meet us down at the dock, and then we buzzed the drive through for some coffee. The drive-thru person acted speechless when I ordered 11 coffees. Driving around with a van full of children, I am quite used to amazed drive-thru clerks who act like they can't hear. I patiently explained that yes, I wanted 11 large coffees. E-L-E-V-E-N. Finally they told us to go through and wait in their parking lot until they brewed another pot or two. Really, it shouldn't be so outrageous to want eleven coffees; they probably sell hundreds in a normal morning.

Finally with the coffees in hand we headed down to the dock. We arrived as the guys were cleaning up the last of the fish. They had several ice chests packed with filets. Later I heard the whole church had a fish fry. Sounds like fun! We'll have to keep that in mind for River of Life.

After I launched the boat, Marlin went and parked the van and trailer, while I started the motor and let it warm up. As Marlin walked up to the dock he asked why my boat had so much water in the back of it. Sure enough, there was water halfway up the batteries in the back. It appeared I had forgotten to put the plug in the boat. I quickly located a plug and put it in the boat, while Marlin retrieved the van and boat trailer. After we pulled the boat back out of the water, it took almost ten minutes to drain everything. I decided now would be a bad time to mention my theory on boat disasters.

Soon we were cruising out of Homer heading for Marlin Eicher's halibut spot. After about thirty minutes, we arrived and dropped anchor. It was very foggy, and I hoped no boats would run into us. Every now and then one would come out of the fog, but they never got really close. We did catch some halibut, but unfortunately I have forgotten who caught what. None of them were enormous, or I would remember. I wanted to show Marlin the bay loaded with salmon, and because entry to the bay is very time sensitive we pulled anchor early and headed that way.

As we cruised along I noticed what looked like a killer whale dorsal fin. I figured this was unlikely as probably the only way to find killer whales was to go on high priced cruises. Soon we noticed more dorsal fins, and suddenly there were killer whales all over the place. We kept our distance, as most of them are bigger than our whole boat. It was right about this time the boat alarm started beeping. I absolutely hate hearing boat alarms. If I am sleeping, and you want to give me a nightmare just play a recording of a boat alarm.

I do sometimes learn from my mistakes. Immediately I shut down the boat motor, then connected my smart phone to the motor's information center. It connects via bluetooth and is the slickest thing. The engine had run hot. We checked the motor, and it looked like a piece of kelp had gotten stuck in the engine water intake. This was quickly removed, and I restarted the engine, keeping tabs on it with my smartphone. With fresh water now going through the system, it cooled down quickly and no harm was done.

It was a relief to clear up this problem and get on with the trip. But no sooner had I gotten up to cruising speed when the alarm started beeping again. This was very concerning, even more so when I looked back and noticed the back of the boat was full of smoke! Again I quickly cut the engine power. Richard and Marlin seemed very concerned and were frantically looking about for a fire extinguisher. In fact I had never before seen Richard so worked up. Right away I noticed the source of our problem. A metal bracket with rubber "muffs" that is used to connect a garden hose to the engine had fallen across the battery post and the metal floor. Half the metal bracket was red hot and part of the rubber was burning. Quickly I grabbed the non burning end and pitched the whole thing overboard, ending the problem. Even more concerning was, this fire had occurred within a few inches of a rubber fuel line.

For awhile after this I puzzled over what set off the engine alarm. Later I realized that because the battery was grounded, the voltage dropped. The engine alarm sounded as a result of low voltage. I looked up the alarm history on the boat motor's computer, and it confirmed what I thought. The boat has two batteries, and I thank the Lord we were running on the same battery that was shorted out. Otherwise the alarm would not have been set off, and we may have ended up swimming with the Orcas.

After this short scare, we were happy to be cruising along again. Finding the little salmon bay was easy now that I had marked it in my GPS. Entering the channel that connects the bay, we tied the boat off on the bank and all disappeared into the woods to use the facilities. While Marlin was waiting on some of us to return he threw his line out and nailed a salmon on the first cast. I think he had two fish in the boat before we even entered the bay. Because we had entered as early as possible on the rising tide we got hung up several times. All we needed to do was just wait a few minutes, and the tide would pick up and carry us further in. I really hated the thought of getting hung up on the way out, with a falling tide! My boat is too heavy to carry!

The action was fast and heavy. The biggest problem was getting the last fish out of the net in time to grab the next one coming in. It only took about twenty minutes to limit out our boat, and that was mostly because we were sharing fishing rods. No foolishness of running out of hooks this time around! I was well equipped. Every time a hook would rip off, we would just laugh and reach into a huge bag full of hooks. In fact, months later as I write this there are still snagging hooks laying all over the boat. Every now and then one will fall out of a compartment, or I will find one stuck under a seat.

Above: Myself and Richard with a small halibut. Above Right: Richard takes photos of Orcas.

Right: The only picture I have from that particular day with Marlin in it. I wasn't trying to exclude him, I guess I was focusing more on running the boat and less on pictures that day.

We returned to the dock and congratulated ourselves on a good day of fishing. I helped Marlin throw some fish in a bag; I think I tossed in an extra one for good measure. This almost got Marlin in trouble later, as he was cleaning his fish at the public cleaning station. Someone said to him, "Whoa--you got seven fish instead of six!" Six is the limit in that area. I'm not sure what Marlin did or said, but he didn't get arrested or fined, so he must have explained the situation well.

Back in Clam Gulch we went about cleaning the fish. I wanted to set up the vacuum packer in the garage, but I couldn't find a close outlet. Finally I just found an extension cord and plugged it in with that. After it was set up, I hit the power switch to power on the vacuum packer. There was a flash of sparks, and the breaker flipped as I got knocked backwards by a jolt of electricity. This caused me to give a loud yell. Nothing like a blast of electric to get things moving. Marlene immediately came out into the garage and demanded to know who was shouting foul language. Thankfully Richard and Shane were both witnesses. They said I had not shouted any words at all, but rather gibberish that made no sense in any language. The culprit was a frayed extension cord that caused a short somewhere. I had run across the cord a few days earlier and set it aside, planning to repair it. After this incident it got thrown in the trash. The breaker was reset, and we did get our fish packed, although we used a different extension cord.

One humorous incident that I must mention before moving on. At church one morning a visitor told Richard that he heard a pack of wolves out behind the house and they "must have just killed something and were fighting over it." Richard just nodded, knowing full well it was our Siberian Huskies and Malamutes he heard howling. The visitor shouldn't feel bad, the plumber and oil man also both thought I had a pack of wolves running loose, and they even live in Alaska.

All good things must come to an end, and so did Richard and Karen's stay in Alaska. I hinted at the finer points of living in Alaska, but Richard seemed impervious to moving. He did promise to come visit often. On the way to the airport we got stuck in a serious traffic jam. This was pretty concerning. If you don't arrive in time your tickets turn to dust. We noticed something up ahead that was smoking furiously. Finally, after sitting almost 45 minutes, traffic started to move again. The cause of the traffic jam was a car that had started on fire and burned to nothing. I don't have anything against lighting cars on fire, but next time pick an abandoned parking lot or something to do it in.

Richard's made it to the airport with a few minutes to spare, and we sent them on their way with 50 pounds of fillets. A big perk of visiting Alaska is almost everyone goes home with hundreds of dollars worth of free fish. Another bit of trivia: Richards were heading home to attend Ira Petershiem's wedding. Ira was up working on our cabin in Book 2, on the same occasion when Josh ended up spending $800 to get home a few hours earlier for a first date. Ira married Alison Martin. Both Ira and Alison attended Crossroads Mennonite Church, where we attended while living in Pennsylvania.

Above: Next time I hope this fellow picks another place to burn his car. I'm surprised it was-
n't a PT Cruiser. Below: All the children on the hill in front of the Homer Spit.

Chapter 42
Marlene's Parents Visit Alaska

I had tried for several weeks to sell Emmanuel Esh's Dodge pickup truck. The truck was indeed very nice, a 2500 series with a Cummins diesel. I only drove it once, because without a doubt it would get wrecked, had I driven it more. Had the truck been four wheel drive I could have probably sold it six or seven times. But nobody wants a two wheel drive truck in Alaska. Emmanuel started getting restless, and rightly so. Had the truck been four wheel drive I would have even considered buying it. A two wheel drive vehicle (especially in Alaska) reminds me of the unfaithful man in Proverbs 25:19: Confidence in an unfaithful man in time of trouble is like a broken tooth, and a foot out of joint.

Finally we came upon a solution: Marlene's parents, John and Mary Martin, would fly up and drive the truck back to Pennsylvania. Shockingly, they were a little cool to the idea at first. Who wouldn't want a free 4,000+ mile road trip? Marlene's dad seemed particularly suspicious of the vehicle. I assured him that it wasn't my truck, and that helped him feel a little better about the idea. After sending him some pictures of the truck, he agreed to bring it back to Pennsylvania.

So it was, that they came to visit Alaska again. Last time they were up to visit they stayed in our old Fleetwood camper in Anchor Point. They ended up sleeping in the cabin because they were convinced the RV was going to explode due to a gas leak or some minor flaw somewhere. Or, maybe it was the fumes blowing into the camper from the generator parked outside the door that perked their concern. They are into natural remedies and organic things, so they naturally shy away from exhaust fumes. I'm not sure if those events played into their reluctance to return to Alaska, but they did seem relieved that we had a "normal" house now.

John and Mary flew into Anchorage and we picked them up. I was eager to have John here, as I was hoping he could fix some of my vehicles. I sensed a little less enthusiasm coming from him, but he did agree to see what he could do. First I had him fix the brakes on my white van. It seemed the one rear brake assembly had completely came loose from the axle. We drove it anyway, as three brakes are more than enough, but all the rattling and grinding noises got on my nerves. After fixing that up, he took a look at my truck.

As I explained earlier, my truck loved to throw off its oil line, and then pump all the oil out on the ground. It was like a spoiled child, always doing something for attention. John crawled under the truck and decided to take a look. After some fiddling and wrenching he managed to remove the offending oil line. We spent the rest of the day driving around looking for another one, but to no avail. The replacement parts could not be located.

Shane, John, and myself stopped by Walmart to grab some dog food. John seemed astounded by the amount of dog food we got, but hey, the dogs have to eat too. I didn't want to waste all John and Mary's time fooling around with vehicles, so we also did some sightseeing. After a few days they got into Emmanuel's truck and headed back to Pennsylvania. They seemed to be sure something awful would happen, but the truck performed well (except both rear brakes failed), and they made good time. It was nice to have the truck out of the way, and Emmanuel was equally happy to have it back.

Buying dog food at Walmart. I wonder if they noticed their sales of this particular brand skyrocketing.

Above: John seeks to fix the troublesome Chevrolet pickup. Beside him is the offending oil hose. Below: Sweet corn! Who says we can't have sweet corn in Alaska?!

Above: Grandpa (John) and I must have worked too hard that day fixing the truck and hauling dog food.

Right: Grandma (Mary) is still full of energy. The children seem to enjoy her visit.

Chapter 43
Marlene Goes Fishing

It is safe to say that Marlene is not as fond of boats as I am. However, I did have her approval for the new four stroke motor. I felt bad for doing all this fishing without her, and finally one day I convinced her to go along fishing. We planned the trip out a few days in advance. First we would go to our secret little salmon bay, then head over to Seldovia for lunch. After that we would bag a few halibut, and then head back to Homer. To increase our limits we decided to take Shane, Kallia, Lana and Mary Kate along. The rest of the children were babysat; I think by Karen Eicher.

Mary Kate tends to get worked up in situations where there is a lot of noise or action. For example, she panicked when the airplane took off on our way to Nome. So I was a little dubious about taking her along fishing, but she has to get over her fear sometime. Sure enough, when we took off out of Homer on the boat she started getting scared. "Let me out!" she begged as we roared across the water. Needless to say, we didn't comply with her wishes. After a few minutes she settled down and was happy with the boat ride.

We rolled into our little salmon bay right on time, not even getting hung up at the entrance. There were even more fish here than the last few times we tried it! Marlene and Shane started hauling in fish after fish. It was a little tricky getting the younger children to catch them, but they loved it. Where else can you haul in large salmon, one after the other, until your arms get tired out? We left before we had our limit because everyone was complaining their arms were tired. Besides, we already had more salmon at home in the freezer than we knew what to do with.

On our way over to Seldovia we stopped and tried a little halibut fishing. Everyone was hungry, so we cut this short. There was a 400 foot deep hole I wanted to try and fish, but I decided we would just have to get it later on another trip. Despite what Marlene tries to say, she has an adventurous side and was excited to see the town of Seldovia.

Last time I docked at Seldovia with Jerry, I tied the boat up at the wrong spot. This time I knew where to go and nicely tied up like someone who knew what he was doing. Then we signed in at the harbor master office. We walked up and down the streets for awhile before deciding where to eat. The restaurant overlooked the harbor. It was a rather nifty feeling to be eating at a boat or fly-in only town and looking out the window at our boat tied up in the harbor.

I discovered quickly that nobody goes to Seldovia to save money on lunch. The menu prices were rather salty, and a 12 oz can of soda was $3. We ended up ordering water, but they cleverly made the water taste terrible (maybe it was pumped straight from the ocean), and we ended up buying a few high priced soft drinks. On the bright side the food was good, probably because if they served bad food at those prices it would cause a riot.

After eating we walked around the town for awhile. We asked about bringing a vehicle over on the ferry, but if we did, it would be stuck there for two weeks (the ferry only goes every other week). Sometime our family might come for a week and explore the town. Maybe we'll just buy a bigger boat and end up camping out in the harbor, as I'm sure the motels are expensive. If we want to really save money we'll get a boat large enough to fit a four wheeler on, saving us the expense of renting one. Seldovia also has an airstrip, so perhaps we can someday fly over in a plane.

We had not yet caught any halibut, but the family was getting restless and wanted to go back. Of course we had no bathroom on the boat, and this provided for some difficult situations. It was an enjoyable day, and we all made some good memories.

Below: Not bad for an outing fishing with the family. For reference, the table below is four feet wide. We caught more fish that day but these are the largest ones.

Above: It is fairly unusual to find Marlene holding a fishing rod.
Below: Lana caught a couple of nice salmon.

Above: Our boat is parked in the middle of the window. Can you see it?

Below: Heading to downtown Seldovia.

Above and Below: Downtown Seldovia! It is worth the boat (or plane) ride to visit this small rather picturesque community.

Chapter 44
Andrew Stoltzfus's Boat Breaks Down

Like almost all the members of our church, Andy was trying to build his house that summer. I had offered to help him but had never got around to it. One evening Andy called and wondered if I wanted to make good on my promise to help him build by going fishing. I'm not good at building and tend to enjoy fishing somewhat, so I was eager to learn more. Some folks from somewhere (I think maybe Kentucky) were up visiting Alaska, and they had offered to help Andy with his house construction. Andy was hoping to take them on a fishing trip as a token of thanks. But his boat was small, he could only take four or five people, and they all wanted to go at once. His boat was actually my old boat that I had sold him the year before. I agreed to make the sacrifice of fishing instead of doing physical construction work.

At 5 A.M. I left Clam Gulch, once again wondering what was wrong with me for getting up so early. I also figured that we wouldn't catch any fish. Usually if I take people out hoping to impress them, it is a disaster. Upon meeting Andy and his friends in Homer, we proceeded to launch our boats. Andy launched his with his motorhome. I guess that is no worse than using a limo to launch. Before leaving the dock I informed the group of guys that I was not a charter, and I didn't expect or want any payment. If Fish and Game think you are running a charter without the proper licenses you can get in big trouble and your boat confiscated. Note to everyone: I don't run a fishing charter, and I don't ever plan to. If you want to go fishing in Alaska, call a charter well ahead of time. Don't show up at my doorstep with tears in your eyes saying how you didn't know better, or I'll be tempted to slap you. Basically what you're doing is either asking me for a free fishing trip, or asking me to break the law and have my boat confiscated and fined thousands of dollars. With that said, I do occasionally take visitors fishing, but if I admitted that, my door would be overrun with tourists wanting free fishing trips.

Andy decided to head over to China Poot bay with his group of guys and try some salmon snagging, and the rest of us went about a mile off the dock to try and get some halibut. I punched in the same spot that worked well other times that I discovered in 2015 when Conrad Brubaker's were visiting. I didn't go far, because the boat was near or over it's weight limit: six people. Not to mention only a few of the folks were particularly thin. The boat handled terribly, and I wouldn't have even considered going with that many except the sea was calm as glass. In the future I don't think I will even take a group that size in calm waters.

Some of the guys told me they hadn't caught a fish in years and doubted they would this time. That was a relief; at least they wouldn't be disappointed, I thought. To everyone's shock, one of the no-fish-in-years guys

Above: Halibut fishing near the Homer spit. We landed several that day. Below: Towing Andrew Stoltzfus and his boat back to the dock. Thankfully we later discovered he was only out of gas.

was the first one to land a halibut. He seemed elated and very excited. We caught a few more fish, and then the no-fish-in-years guy caught a second halibut! He seemed to think this was an impossibility, like gravity and time had just been reversed.

In the meantime Andy called me. He was down at China Poot Bay, and his engine conked out. Sadly I told everyone we would fish for a few more minutes, then head over to pull Andy back. But before we got our lines in, Andy called again and said that he had gotten his motor started. It would only run with the choke set on full. He had a forty horsepower Evinrude two stroke which normally had been very reliable. As I pondered this I remembered that I had brought some gas along from Pennsylvania the year before and must have put some in the boat. Pennsylvania gas is riddled with ethanol, a substance designed to break down and ruin your carburetor. Because there are no cornfields for thousands of miles, somehow Alaska got off the hook from the ethanol gas requirements. I imagine it is only a matter of time until they discover something equally as harmful to add to the gasoline up here, but for now I'll enjoy having good gas.

Environmentalists may be pleased to know I once attempted to run my old Ford van on corn oil. Years ago I worked at Glenwood Foods in Hinkletown, Pennsylvania. For some reason that remains unknown, there was about twenty gallons of corn oil in the trash truck. I took the liberty of dumping some of this into my fuel tank. Times were tough, and I figured maybe I could stretch my gasoline "budget" (the amount of money in my pocket at the moment) a bit further by doing this. I had heard of people running vehicles on corn oil. It turns that out the people that did this all had diesel engines. Gasoline and corn oil are not similar at all. The van still did run, but every now and then, for months afterwards, it would go into periodic spells of running very rough, belching smoke. If you were going about five miles an hour it would sometimes buck and lurch dreadfully. I decided from that point on I didn't want to put vegetable products in my fuel tank.

Our time for halibut fishing was up, and it was time to go back to the dock. I hadn't heard anything from Andy and was startled, but not altogether surprised, to come upon him paddling his boat. We threw him a line and gave him a tow back the rest of the way to the dock.

Later Andy took his carburetor apart. Indeed it was full of gunk. He gave it a good cleaning, and it has worked well ever since. This made me happy, as I hated to think I had sold Andy something that was a lemon. The real reason his engine had completely stopped running? He was out of gas!

Chapter 45
Dipnetting

In Alaska, July means dipnetting. In the off chance you haven't read any of my earlier books, dipnetting is an efficient way to go salmon fishing. It involves putting huge nets over the side of a boat and cruising along slowly. Before long (hopefully) your net starts to shake, and you pull a nice salmon in. You beat it over the head, slit the gills, and toss it in the fish compartment. Then you catch another one! This all depends on how the salmon are running. Some days are great, some days are terrible. You won't know until you try it. Other years I was limited to begging for rides in other people's boats. This was because two-stroke engines are illegal on the Kenai River. But suddenly this year I had a four stroke motor. The world was full of possibilities!

A quick note on how and what dipnetting is. Dip Nets are huge circular nets, measuring about three feet across. You motor along slowly, going about 2-3 mph. Salmon get scooped into the nets and thrash around, letting you know you have a fish. The net is then brought overboard, the fish dumped out, and the net put back into the water. Typically the net will get caught on about five other things in the boat, and usually while trying to untangle the mess the other net will also catch a fish. As you frantically try and untangle the first mess, the other person will shout, "I'm going to lose this one if I don't bring it in NOW!" and fling their fish into the boat. More than once I have been hit on the head by flying salmon. Often I also have been "fish slapped" by slimy wet fish tails. I don't mind; this means we are catching fish! The fish are beat over the head with a stout stick, then the gills are slit, the tails are cut (to show they were dip netted-thus can't be sold), and then they are thrown in an ice chest. On a successful day the floor of the boat becomes a sheet of fish slime, and you can barely walk, let alone fling huge nets and wield sharp knives. It is great fun! After a good evening of dipnetting you smell "fishy" for a good day or two. The limit for dipnetting is 25 salmon for the head of the house, and 10 more for each additional family member. This means we could legally catch 105 salmon by means of dipnetting that season.

We went dipnetting twice that summer, both with good success. The first time we went was Wednesday, July 26. The first few weeks of the season were slow as the run was late that year, so we decided to wait until the end. Like many things involving salt water (you can only dipnet close to the mouth of Kenai River) it revolves around the tides. We launched from the Kenai dock, which is closed at low tide because there is no water at the dock! This means if you time your dipnetting wrong you will be stuck somewhere out in the river until the tide comes back in, pushing the level of the river

Above: Marlin's crew hauling in a fish. Below: Filleting salmon at Paul's place. Paul and Makayla graciously helped.

up. Isn't Alaska great? Nothing is for the faint of heart--you come back at the wrong time, and you can't reach the dock. You're out hiking, and you might get mauled by giant bears, or if you're fishing you might run into Orcas larger than your boat. You might get taken down by a pack of wolves if you're not careful. Also blizzards, arctic -50 degree cold, earthquakes and volcanoes might do you in! Fishing involves ice chests full of meat. Nothing is mediocre in Alaska except the squirrels (they look like overgrown chipmunks).

The first day we went dipnetting we ran into a problem. We didn't own any dip nets! Briefly I thought about calling Marlin and trying to borrow his. But just recently I had borrowed his trailer and skid loader. I was a little worried about being misunderstood as a moocher. Not wanting to miss out on the free fish, we went to Mike's Welding in Sterling and dropped $350 for two dip nets. We thought about just buying one, but if you do that you end up going in circles, as the drag of having a net over the side is significant. One net on each side creates the same amount of drag.

Thankfully Marlene agreed to go along. It is easier to convince her to go boating since the new motor was installed. She seemed to be a bit gun shy before that. Our first night dipnetting we got 20 something salmon, which wasn't bad. We were out fishing when suddenly a boat roared up. Here it was Gareth Byers and some other guys from Sterling. Gareth held up a huge King Salmon. "We got two of these this evening!" he said. The one weighed 38 pounds, and the other one I forget. I think the 38 pound king was the small one of the two. I don't know how many salmon they caught, but knowing them, they didn't go back in until they had their limit.

Soon after meeting Gareth, we encountered Marlin, along with his girls Judy and Rose (it's good I didn't ask to borrow his dip nets). I believe Joe Troyer was also along. They were having a good evening and had quite a few salmon on board. We quit around 10:00 P.M., as Shane and Marlene were complaining about being tired out. After that we headed over to Paul and Jo's place in Sterling. Then we stayed up for what seemed like a long time cleaning fish. I think we arrived home well after 1:00 A.M. It was good to get home early for a change.

The next dipnetting trip, on July 28, was with Marcus Yoder and his son Kasper. Marc runs Northstar Metals in Soldotna and also attends Sterling Mennonite Church. Once again we headed out in the evening, as that favored high tide. The salmon were running strong and hard. We nailed fish after fish! We caught 71 salmon that evening.

That evening Marlene was staying with Marc's wife, Dorcas. I texted Marlene a running total of the fish we caught. At first her texts we congratulatory. "Good job!" or "Way to go!" were typical responses. As our success increased, her exuberance started quickly dropping. She started sending messages like "Stop! Come back," "Argggh!," "Horrors! we will be up all

Left: Kasper Yoder inspects our haul of salmon, and the evening is not over yet! That is a 120 quart ice chest.

Below: An ice chest full of sockeye (red) salmon fillets! Fresh salmon runs $20+ a pound, and here we have an ice chest so loaded we can hardly lift it. It is illegal for us to sell these however.

Below left: Canned salmon! Don't pass any chances to try salmon dip made from canned salmon, it is the best. We also vacuumed packed lots of salmon. I got these fancy stickers made up to put on the packs.

Wild Alaska Caught
Salmon
Captain Matt's
Summer/Fall 2017 Not for Sale

night cleaning fish!" It is hard to reason with men who are fishing and actually catching droves of fish. Marc, Kasper, Shane, and myself were unstoppable. However nearing 11 P.M. our arms began to ache. One can only scoop so many fish out of the river at once.

Towards the end of the evening the boat began to handle terribly. I worried that we might be taking on some water and not realizing it, or perhaps the engine was not making power like I thought it should. Later I realized that with 71 salmon averaging 8 pounds each, we would have had 568 pounds of just fish onboard. This was in addition to two men (who undoubtedly were very fit and trim) and Casper and Shane, and all our tackle. The boat weight limit is 800 some pounds of cargo (people and tackle), which meant we were hundreds of pounds overweight. Our large ice chest was packed with fish, the live well was packed with fish, and there were dozens of fish all over the bottom of the boat. It was truly a memorable evening.

As we loaded the boat up at the dock, the realization of what we had done began to set in. Inside the boat were over 70 salmon, 500 pounds of fish, that needed to be cleaned! We decided with that kind of work ahead of us we needed some nourishment. Unfortunately Arby's closed just as we pulled in. We headed down the road to McDonalds, but unfortunately everyone else who was dipnetting went there too. We waited half an hour for some french fries and burgers. What complicated the matter was we requested our food to be made without salt. This requires the crew to make fresh food for you, because normally salt is added. I think perhaps the workers detected our little ploy and carefully set the salt free food back to age a little before serving it. After all, what are the odds of everyone in a group of four ordering all their food without salt? The fact Marc requested little packets of salt didn't help.

After the painfully long wait we headed back to Marc's to fillet the fish. Marc and Dorcas graciously offered to let us clean all the fish at their place. For some reason, whenever I am cleaning fish it is always in the middle of the night and marginally above freezing. As we slaved away, fish after fish, the sky gradually grew lighter. Finally around 5 A.M. we cleaned the last fish. With one eye open I drove back to Clam Gulch. It is a wonder I didn't get pulled over for a D.U.I. check. After throwing some ice on the fillets we went to bed for a few hours.

The fun doesn't stop with cleaning the fish, though. You need to process the fillets by freezing or canning them. In this case we did both. Marlene set to work canning, and I set to work vacuum packing. We had decided to can the fish without skin, meaning we had to carefully cut the skin off each fillet. This idea sounded good at first, but after a few dozen fillets I was about to give up the idea.

As we staggered around the kitchen, mounds of fish skin, fillets, and general debris everywhere, Shane announced someone had stopped in. Through half closed eyes I wondered who it could be. It was a family from Pennsylvania stopping in to visit. They are fans of our books and wanted to stop in and say hi. I have tried hard to remember their names without avail, so if you're the family and reading this please forgive me for not including you. They had modified a regular enclosed trailer into a camper. Not once had they stopped at a hotel or restaurant on the entire trip! That's what I call saving money. I, of course always travel this way too, except on the off occasion when I get hungry or tired. We weren't in a position to be very hospitable that afternoon, but we did talk for awhile, and I made sure they didn't leave without some salmon and halibut.

Below: Gareth with the two impressive king salmon that they caught in dipnets. He said they really made the net go wild!

Chapter 46
BuckEyePuppies.com visits Alaska

Readers may remember some mentions of Leon Beachy from Ohio in previous books. Leon originally was in charge of the office in Ohio, a division of Online Advertising (LancasterPuppies.com) known as Buck-EyePuppies.com. Leon now runs the entire Online Advertising set of websites. The most well known are LancasterPuppies.com, BuckEyePuppies.com, and the camouflage limo wielding AmericanGunDogs.com. Because we wanted to start advertising operations in Alaska, I invited Leon to come up and help out. Of course he brought his wife, Trista, and their daughter Genesis along.

Our first appointment was at Marc Yoders. They started raising English Bulldogs. In fact one of the first times I met Marc he casually mentioned he got his Bulldog off of LancasterPuppies.com. He had purchased it out of Pennsylvania and had it transported up by United Airlines. I figured Marc was just telling me this because I was a part of Online Advertising, but later Marc told me he had no idea I had anything to do with it. His bulldog now had puppies, so we listed them for him on our websites.

We took Leon and Tris hiking one day at Fuller Lakes trail. This trail goes up a mountainside for several miles. Previously we had tried to hike it but forgot to bring water along. The previous time, much to everyone's chagrin, I drank water straight out of a stream. I never got sick, and I suspect the water was higher quality than what we normally drank. But nobody else wanted to drink out of the creek, so we ended up quitting before we reached the lakes at the top. This time we wanted to hike the whole way up. We brought along plenty of water and of course, a few guns. The hike was beautiful, but uneventful.

On another day we took Leon and Tris to see the Russian River falls. Salmon climb these falls to get to their spawning grounds. You can stand there and watch fish after fish leap up through the waterfall. No wonder they are about dead by the time they reach the spawning grounds. There were plenty of tired salmon puttering about under the falls, and I had to talk Shane out of trying to catch them with his hands.

Somewhere along the trail we scared up a moose and calf. They took off running down the trail as only moose do. However they would only run a short distance, then stop. We would soon catch up to them, and then Leon would run after them again. I was a tiny bit concerned Leon might get stomped on, but he didn't seem worried. Tris seemed very worried and was relieved when the moose finally wandered off into the woods.

Leon brought his drone along to Alaska, and we had fun flying it around the water. Fortunately he avoided all the trees. Leon was the first person to introduce me to drones, and I have been fascinated with them ever since.

Above: Group photo with our family and Leon and Trista and their daughter Genesis. Below: The boardwalk, observation areas, and the Russian River falls.

Chapter 47
Expedition to Port Chatham

For years I have yearned to visit the allegedly Bigfoot-infested shores of Port Chatham and put to rest my curiosity. Alaska and the Internet is full of wild stories about this place. It all started with a cannery going out of business in the 1940's. Legend has it this cannery went out of business due to the villagers (who all worked for the cannery) packing up and all leaving at once. This occurred because allegedly they got tired of getting torn to pieces by some monster lurking in the woods (another very boring rumor is the cannery went bankrupt). This monster legend was a Bigfoot, Sasquatch, or whatever you want to call it. Of course scientists denounce the existence of this type of creature, making it all the more intriguing. If scientists said, "Yes, this exists, but it hides most of the time", I would probably forget all about it and chalk it up as boring. After all, how many people talk in hushed tones about monkeys. I'm just waiting for Bigfoot to be tied to climate change or evolution. Of course, if they make that link, scientists will say there is no doubt it exists, no evidence needed.

Port Chatham is over fifty miles from the dock of Homer. This presented several logistical challenges. First was fuel. My boat can barely get to Port Graham and back without running out of gas. Port Chatham was quite a ways further, almost as far as Elizabeth Island. A second, more concerning problem was the issue of weather. There were no towns after Port Graham. If the weather got bad the only recourse was to find a cove and anchor up, or at worst tie the boat off on the shore. Then the only thing to do was sit and wait for the weather to calm down. A third concern was getting killed by Bigfoot, although this one didn't bother us very much.

Early in the morning on August 2nd we launched out of Homer with Leon, Paul, Kirk (Paul's son), Shane, and myself onboard. The boat was heavily loaded with fuel, people, and tackle. Onboard were also several large caliber rifles in case the rumors were true. I had calculated we would need at least 10 extra gallons of gas to make it back. Because I wasn't interested in taking chances I took 15 extra gallons along. I would have preferred taking more, but gas is heavy and flammable. I didn't want more gas along than we needed. We figured on the way back we would check our gasoline stock near Seldovia, and if we were running low we would just head in and buy a few more gallons.

The weather forecast was good, but in Alaska that doesn't mean much. The forecasts are so woefully inaccurate your chance of good weather is probably better if the forecast is bad. Of course we also had halibut tackle onboard. Around Port Graham we took a break for a few minutes and tried some fishing. This proved to be uneventful, and we soon pulled the lines in and headed on south. As we rounded a point five or six miles after Port

Above: The foreboding shore of Port Chatham. Pronounced Chat-ham. Below: Fishing several miles from Port Chatham we discovered a nice halibut hole.

Graham the wind really picked up. Being this close to Port Chatham I didn't want to stop now, and we pushed on. How disappointing it would be to be so close and have to quit because of the weather! The waves became wilder, and I secretly wondered how the trip back might go. I tried to conceal my nervousness from the others by loudly proclaiming the seaworthiness of my craft. Paul and Leon both pointed out that the other boats in the area were much larger. This coincidence didn't interest me.

After crossing some especially rough water and huge beds of floating kelp, we came to a buoy that said Port Chatham on it. Soon after the buoy we noticed whales surfacing. Several times they breached, with most of the whale clearing the water. Of course I missed it with the camera. Flying whales don't stay in the air very long. As soon as we entered the port, it became very foggy, so foggy we could hardly see anything! This was a bit frustrating, as I had waited so long to get here, and now only to see just fog. There was a little spit sticking out of the port that we circled around. A few sticks and what looked like ruins might have been there, but it didn't look very interesting. We circled around the cove and almost ran into rocks. There were rocks everywhere! This made me nervous. Hitting rocks can make a good day of boating go bad quickly. The weather continued to get worse as we circled the cove. It was hard to see anything, and larger than I expected!

Disappointed we exited the cove and tried fishing out front, to see if the weather might clear. Instead of clearing it started to rain buckets. Thankfully we all wore rain gear, but it was still a bit miserable. Finally we packed up and headed north, back the way we had come. Five miles out of Port Chatham the rain calmed down, and we tried fishing again. This time we had success! We discovered a spot where we consistently got bites. Because I didn't feel like dropping anchor we had to keep circling back after drifting.

My experience has been you are just as well off drifting with the tide, but who knows, I'm sure people argue for hours over what method is best. After getting some halibut on board we continued to Port Graham and fished about a mile offshore. Here I noticed the boat was flat on empty, so I poured five gallons of gas in the tank. The fishing continued to be good here. Finally, to everyone's shock and amazement, we had our limit. There was nothing more to do but go home! The rain actually stopped, and the sun came out. It seemed there was a point between Port Graham and Port Chatham that was a dividing line for the weather. I suspect it may have something to do with the mountains and winds aloft or something.

Around Seldovia I checked our fuel reserves and added some more gas. We still had one unused five gallon jug, plus a few gallons in the tank. We continued on without stopping in. As we neared the Homer harbor entrance the boat shut off. We had run out of gas! Thankfully we had some in the gas can yet, so a gallon or two later we were set and made it to the dock. I prided myself on efficient trip planning, although they tell me with airplanes you need to use tighter tolerances.

Everyone was amazed when we arrived home around 6:00 P.M. That day we logged 110 miles on the boat, about the same distance the Marine Tour cruise had taken. Maybe next time I'll just take my boat to Seward instead of hiring some high priced outfit. If I do that I doubt we'll eat freshly prepared prime rib and salmon on the boat ride.

Below: These were all small halibut, but we were happy with them anyway. Sometime I want to connect with a 100 pounder, or maybe even a salmon shark.

Chapter 48
The Salmon Fishing Improves

Like Richard, Leon wanted to return to the secret little cove tucked away off to the side of Cook Inlet. I couldn't blame him, I wanted to go back too. I was worried that sometime I would return, and no fish would be there. Perhaps that will happen sometime, but each time I returned there were more fish there. This time with Leon was no exception. I knew there were a lot of fish at this spot, but when Leon launched his drone we saw something that shocked us. Across the lagoon were literal rivers of salmon! Sure, we could see there were a lot of fish around from the boat, but from the air it was really incredible.

We did the usual limiting out in a few minutes and started to head back. I noticed what looked like a stream of fish on either side of the boat on the fish finder. When I pointed this out to Leon, he made the comment that you could not trust fish finders. Then Leon looked over the edge, and realized the fish finder was not lying. Swimming parallel to the boat, on either side, was a stream of salmon. They were heading into the lagoon while we were heading out.

Below: Literal rives of salmon swimming past the boat.

Above: See those dark spots in the water? That is swarms of salmon.
Below: Our nifty little salmon cove eventually connects to Cook Inlet in the channel leading off into the background.

Chapter 48
Jerry Returns to Alaska!

After returning home to New York from Alaska, Jerry put his finger in a router. Not a computer networking router, but the kind with a blade that cuts things. Because he does woodworking for a living this caused him some time off work. Even before Jerry mauled his finger we had discussed how profitable it could be to drive old, cheap motorhomes to Alaska for resale. Most of this was theoretical, looking at prices on Craigslist.

Jerry decided that since he couldn't work anyway, he might as well make some money and drive a motorhome up for resale. I did caution him that sometimes plans don't unfold as we wish, but sometimes work out better than expected, and money falls from the sky. Soon Jerry was emailing me pictures of motorhomes. The first few were lackluster, but he did happen up-on one that seemed to be a good deal. It only had 11,000 or some miles on it, but it was a 1996 model. That is pretty old for a motorhome. I cautioned Jer-ry to make sure the roof wasn't rotten. It was a Holiday Rambler, 36 feet long with a slide out. It came equipped with a gas guzzling 460 cubic inch Ford V -8. My Fleetwood (which was a 1994) had the same engine and always ran well, except for using enormous amounts of fuel.

After carefully looking over the Holiday Rambler Jerry decided to buy it. To increase the potential trip profit he also purchased two enclosed trailers and put one inside the other. I was impressed with his desire to make this trip worthwhile. Jerry also wanted to make the trip quick. Right there I noticed a problem. "Quick" and driving a 36 foot motorhome from New York to Alaska, pulling two enclosed trailers, do not belong in the same sentence. Jerry assured me he would bring another fellow along named Steve, and they would just drive nonstop like maniacs the whole way here. I was a bit dubious of that part of the plan, but figured if he did arrive a few days late it wouldn't hurt anything. Since I would be the one reselling the motorhome (for Jerry) we titled it in my name with an Alaska title. This involved mailing some things back and forth but was not a big deal.

Since Jerry was coming this way anyway I ordered a 12,000 watt generator and had it shipped to his house. You wouldn't believe how much it costs to ship something like that to Alaska. I also asked Jerry to bring along two gallons of New York state maple syrup.

Above: The 1996 Holiday Rambler on display for Jerry to look at. Only 11,000 miles, the tires have good tread, what could possibly go wrong?

Below: Jerry is all set to leave his house in western New York. I imagine someday he will also move his family to Alaska.

Chapter 49
Chicago Strikes Again!

As promised, Jerry and Steve did make good time! For the first day they would send updates. "Reached the Ohio line." or "Crossing through so and so town in Indiana." I started to think perhaps they would make the trip in their four day projected window. Then they made the mistake of driving through Chicago.

One early morning I woke up to hear my phone buzz from a text. I briefly thought about ignoring it but looked at it anyway. It was a picture of a motorhome on a lift! "That's strange," I thought. I wondered why Jerry would decide to get the motorhome greased up while on the trip, but I figured everyone has their strange quirks. Maybe a garage had a special deal on oil changes.

A few hours later Jerry texted me. "Can you call me?" the text said. Even though this was Jerry's motorhome, not mine, I got a bad feeling in the pit of my stomach. I was sure he wasn't calling to discuss maintenance schedules.

"Ah, we got a problem here," Jerry told me. The motorhome was leaking transmission fluid, and he took it to a shop. "All it needs is a seal,

and we are good to go," he said. I highly doubted this. Once a transmission starts acting up, they almost always go for broke. In my whole life I have never heard of anyone saying a transmission repair was cheaper than they expected. I encouraged him to have it thoroughly checked out before going further. I doubt towing a motorhome is cheap.

Sure enough, despite having only 11,000 miles the transmission was shot. Sitting around too much had gummed something up, causing it fail. The fluid leak was caused by a bad bearing, which had it been ignored, would have ended up cracking the transmission case. This would have meant mega money repairs.

As I totally expected Jerry called me again a few hours later. The motorhome did need a seal in the transmission, there was no doubt. However the problem was the bad bearing caused a shaft to wobble, which ruined the seal.

With only a new seal, the RV would be good for about twenty miles until it started leaking again. The wobbling shaft would inevitably wobble more and more, until it cracked the transmission housing. More than likely the shaft would also turn sideways, take out every gear and clutch in the transmission, and leave a huge mess lying on the highway. Only replacing the leaking seal was a bad plan. Jerry explained that now they also needed to replace the faulty bearing, which would cost more than the seal. I knew that now that the cycle of transmission failure had swung into motion, there would be no stopping it until it hit rock bottom. Jerry was optimistic that "just a bearing" would do the trick.

Being an optimist I hoped Jerry was right. However I knew that in reality optimists usually are wrong, and the end result would be a financial bloodbath. Sure enough, Jerry called again. "The whole tranny is shot," he said. This cheered me up, as we had hit the bottom and the only way was up, provided of course the engine didn't also fail or roaming gangs didn't loot anything.

Contrary to my expectations, the garage did a remarkable job rebuilding the tranny in short order. Two days later Jerry and Steve were on the road again. Another issue Jerry ran into was he had now maxed out all his credit cards at the transmission shop. He had no room to purchase fuel, as this previously allocated money was used up. Being wise in the matters of finances I advised Jerry to get a new credit card with a fresh limit. He found a Cabela's store, and they eagerly issued him a new credit card. Now he was good to go.

After the transmission episode, everything went well, with one exception. The RV had eight tires. After entering Canada every single tire took a turn failing. Naturally they didn't all go at once, but kept stringing Jerry along. Every few hundred miles there would be another explosion, and then the sound of torn rubber hitting the road. I can relate to this, except most of my flat tire problems have been with small trailers or cars. Changing the tire on a 30,000 pound GVW motorhome is like changing the tire on a heavy truck. The tires are bulky, there are many lugs, and they take a lot of effort to turn on and off.

Once Jerry called me late in the night. They were on the Alcan highway and a few miles earlier they had put on the spare tire, and now it had just blown out. They were stuck without a spare, in the middle of the wilderness. I tried not to panic for them, but I was imagining all sorts of long waits and immense road service bills. But Jerry is innovative and was in hurry, so I figured they might work something out.

The next morning I asked Jerry how things were going. As I expected, they had come up with an improvised solution. Jerry explained that it occurred to him that the dual wheels would work with only one tire. The flat tire was on the tag axle, so they took it off and put the flat tire on the dual axle and moved a good tire from the dual back onto the tag axle. Then they simply cut the flat tire off the rim and bolted it on the dual (because the axle is setup for duals it needed two rims on it). Then they proceeded at 45 mph for the rest of the night until they came to the next town. I think he mentioned they did stop and sleep somewhere in between as well for a few hours.

Finally Jerry and Steve did manage to make it the whole way to Alaska. They arrived at our place on the evening of August 5, having left New York early in the morning on August 2. A very impressive run, considering all the interruptions along the way!

Chapter 50
Jerry Wraps Up The House Trim

On Monday morning Jerry started working on our house trim. I think the real reason he returned was he felt bad about leaving some loose ends. He knew that if I tried to finish up the trim the house would never look the same.

Unselfishly, I also took Jerry and Steve fishing. Of course this was for their benefit. Due to the stress they experienced driving up, it was imperative they did something relaxing. I view fishing as preventive maintenance for a host of health problems. In fact, I figure that the cost of fishing is more than offset by medical bills you avoid. The more fish you catch, the more relaxed you are, so it pays to have good equipment.

Jerry managed to nail a nice fifty pound halibut but didn't catch any octopuses this time around. Steve caught a tire kicker or two. A day later Jerry and Steve both left on flights back East. I do hope they come again soon. Jerry did leave the motorhome at my place, with the words, "you can use it until it sells." I wonder if he thought that statement through.

Below: The inside of the motor home. Not bad, if I do say so myself.

Above: Our nice catch of halibut. The big one stretches out on either side of the four foot wide table. Below: Those fish made a lot of fillets!

Chapter 51
Goat Hunting With Luis

Shane had pulled a goat tag for the area above Halibut Cove, which is almost directly across from the Homer Spit. This cove is where Andrew Stoltzfus and I saw the whales in Book 3, and the same place Marlin Swarey and I went fishing in Book 3. It used to be the far reaches for my first boat, but now with my bigger boat is just a short jog out of Homer. I like this trend. Who knows where we will end up next...Dutch Harbor? No, probably not for a long time. Anyway Luis asked me if Shane and I would consider going hunting with him. Luis has a goat tag for the same area as Shane. I wasted no time saying yes for several reasons. First, Luis is skilled at hunting. He also is great at skinning animals and is much more fit than myself. It was all a downside for him to take me along, except that I had a boat. The only way to get to Halibut Cove was by a boat. Proverbs 18:24 says, "A man that hath friends must shew himself friendly." I have found a boat to also be a helpful item in collecting friends.

Friday, August 18, was our planned hunt date. The evening before we left I went over the boat, checking the batteries and making sure everything was in place. I noticed my new Lowrance GPS with the 3D imaging sonar. This device wasn't the cheapest thing I had ever purchased, and I wouldn't need 3D imaging just to head over to Halibut Cove. The boat already had an older Hummingbird GPS unit that would work fine. Knowing the boat would likely be parked unattended for most of the day I decided to remove the unit. It came out with only a few bolts and someone could easily just help themselves. So I pulled the unit out and set it on the side of the boat. Then I connected the battery charger, just to top off the batteries and went to bed. We planned to leave around 5 A.M. the next morning.

I was awakened shortly after five by a text on my phone. Luis said he was running late! After chiding him on his tardiness, I ran around like a lunatic getting dressed. Shane groggily wandered out of his room, and we were actually ready by the time Luis arrived. We were using Luis's truck that day, as Marlene didn't want to be stuck at home. My truck was still broken down and clogging up the driveway. The limo was also still broken down. So, it was Luis's truck or we were not going at all.

As we rattled down the Sterling Highway towards Ninilchik, I suddenly had a terrible thought. I could not remember putting my Lowrance sonar device in the garage. It was probably still perched on the side of the boat when we left! I begged Luis to quickly pull over, and he dutifully complied. After he stopped I ran back to the boat. No Lowrance unit was in the boat. Talk about depressing! This 3D scan unit was barely a month old, and my carelessness had probably smashed it to pieces on the highway. It was no use

Above: Shane holds the boat at the dock while we wait for Luis to come back from parking the truck and trailer. Below: Ah, what could be better? Morning at the Homer harbor.

ruining a good day of goat hunting by crying over it, so we continued south.

We managed to launch the boat in decent time, and I even remembered the plug. By now I had Shane trained to remind me every 30 seconds. This habit was downright annoying, and I felt like leaving the plug out on purpose. The trip over to Halibut Cove only took about fifteen minutes. Once there, we had to find the trail head. Hiking in the wilderness without a trail is a trial, especially up the side of a mountain. Thankfully we found the trail without any problems.

The next issue to deal with was tying up the boat. The tide was at the lowest point, and the sea level would rise fifteen feet in the next six or so hours (during the clam tides high tide can be over 25 feet high). This meant we needed to plan our anchor accordingly, or the boat would be pulled under, or rip out the anchor and float off. Both options were bad. Thankfully Luis was well versed on anchor systems and proceeded to lay one out. It involved running huge lengths of rope all over the place, and after awhile I gave up trying to follow the process.

Finally we were ready to hike up the trail. Shane was carrying the .50 Beowulf, and I was using my .300 Winchester Magnum. Luis had a .270. As we hiked, we talked loudly about our various intellectual pursuits. Suddenly, we saw the tail of a bear disappear around the corner. This was very unexpected. We picked up the pace but were not able to catch up to the bear right away. The trail was very winding, steep, and full of switchbacks. Finally we came to a spot where the trail was straight for about a hundred yards. Up ahead stood the bear, as if he didn't have a care in the world. He was actually probably a deranged killer and was thinking how he was going to lure us into an ambush. Luis and I wasted no time both firing at the bear. Even with a .270 bullet and a .300 Winchester Magnum in his system he seemed awfully energetic, and we contemplated sending more bullets his way. However by now we were standing about thirty feet from the bear. Both of us were sure of our shot placement, and we didn't want the hide and meat ruined with multiple bullet holes, so we waited a bit. This turned out to be a wise decision.

Luis and I were ecstatic. Neither one of us had a good deal of experience actually finding big game. It didn't matter we were here to hunt goats, bear season was open all year, and in my opinion bears are just as exciting as goats. As we contemplated what to do next, we heard some people coming down the trail. They were half shouting, half singing, "Bear! Bear! Bear!" They sounded like tourists, trying to prevent maulings by alerting the bears they were there. This might get interesting, as a bear was laying right across the trail, obviously dead. We stood right beside it, brandishing rifles, obviously the killers.

Above: Luis sets up the anchor system, which requires various loops of cord to be run here and there. Below: At times the tide can come the whole way up to the grass, demonstrating the need for a flexible anchor system.

Sure enough, they looked like trouble. The hikers had British accents, and instead of hearty congratulations they appeared distraught as soon as they noticed the dead bear. It was a middle aged lady and a guy, dressed in fancy designer hiking clothes. It was obvious this was the first time something of this nature had occurred to them. Finally the guy found his voice. "Did you shoot the bear in self defense?" he inquired. We told him we had not. It had been running away, and we gunned it down. We planned to eat the bear. This information did not please him. He then questioned if what we were doing was legal, and so forth. The lady didn't say much of anything, but appeared to be on the verge of passing out. Politely we told them that bear season was open. They paused, as if not sure what to say or do. Abruptly they hiked off down the trail, and we never saw them again. I think in their minds we were murderers, and they suddenly thought they were in the middle of no where, arguing with a bunch of gun wielding nuts. If they went to Fish and Game to report us, it would have been hilarious to listen to Fish and Game inform them we were actually law abiding citizens.

We decided to drag the bear down to the boat, since it was all downhill. After gutting the bear, Luis pulled out a bunch of gear, which included a rope (didn't I mention it was good to bring him along?) Pulling the bear down to the boat only took about twenty minutes, and a few times the bear passed us up.

The boat was retrieved, and we hefted the bear into it. I couldn't help but feel more authentic Alaskan every minute, hauling dead bears around in my boat. Everyone jumped in and we headed back to Homer. Not wanting to upset anyone at the dock, we discussed our options. In the end we decided to put a tarp over the bear in case any more non-Alaskans noticed us.

After the boat was loaded we headed back to Clam Gulch. On the way through Anchor Point we swung into Andrew and Tabitha's place. They were delighted and very congratulatory when we showed them the bear. At first they thought we would be showing them some halibut or salmon and were a bit taken aback when they looked in the boat.

At my place Luis once again showed the value of taking him along hunting. He skinned out the bear, all the while apologizing that he wasn't very good at this sort of thing. I personally didn't see anything wrong with his skinning job. He even offered to take the rest of the bear away and butcher it. That sounded good to me, and so our hunting trip was over for that day. Shane was slightly disgruntled he didn't get to shoot at or even see any goats, but I explained that you got to take what you get, or "strike while the iron is hot." People that sit around and whine about things are generally miserable their whole life. Plus, it makes a great excuse to go again, although we never did get to return to Halibut Cove that year. Oh, and the missing Lowrance 3D fish finder? I found it sitting safely on a shelf in my garage. That sure made me happy!

Left: The way Shane is grinning, I can't blame the British folks for being nervous.
Below: Dragging the bear out. It was a pretty heavy bear and required two people to pull it.
Below left: Gutting the bear.

Above: I wouldn't mind giving some more bears a ride in my boat.
Below: Not the most dignified way to show off trophies, but the children seemed to enjoy it, and the bear didn't mind. Noodles was terrified and wouldn't stop barking.

Chapter 52
Marlene, Shane, and Dallas Fly to Pennsylvania

No, Marlene didn't get fed up with Alaska and leave. Our good friends, Shannon and Ann High, still live in Pennsylvania (as I write this they do). Their oldest son, Donovan, is the same age as Shane. Naturally they are good friends. That summer Donovan had surgery on his throat to help him swallow better. The recovery process was taking longer than expected, and Shane wanted to visit. We also figured that both boys would benefit from this. Marlene and I also thought it would be fun if they did this unannounced and surprised everybody. One drawback with these kind of thing is that the people you are going to surprise might just up and go somewhere else (like an impromptu vacation), but if they are in the hospital that is unlikely.

I got tickets for Marlene, Shane, and Dallas to fly into Harrisburg. In order to keep it a surprise for everyone I rented a vehicle at the airport. Vehicle rentals in Harrisburg are affordable in the summer, unlike Alaska. For some odd reason the cheapest vehicle was a four wheel drive pickup. So I rented them a truck, which turned out to be almost brand new. Marlene commented how nice a new truck was, and I told her to not get used to it. Before cruising on out to Snyder County, Pennsylvania, Marlene headed in to Lancaster to surprise my parents. Because Marlene's parents are constantly traveling all over creation with their taxi work, we had given them the heads up. My parents generally do not travel so we figured we could risk surprising them. This was going to be fun!

To set the stage for the surprise I called my mom via Skype. This is a free video service that allows you to see each other on the computer as you talk. This I did for two reasons. One, I wanted to distract my mom while Shane and Marlene sneaked into her house. Two, I wanted to watch her reaction to them walking into the room. As I was talking to my mom, I was texting Marlene with my cell phone. Marlene informed me that they were in the driveway. Because my parents frequently have visitors I figured she wouldn't pay a lot of attention to a vehicle. Sure enough, Mom said, "I hear Pooh Bear (their dog) barking. Your dad and JJ must be back." I knew better but didn't disagree. I kept the conversation going with small talk as I got a text from Marlene, "We are in the house." Eagerly I kept an eye on the door behind my mom.

Marlene and Shane burst through the door. My mom turned her head to see, and her mouth dropped open. "MARLENE!" she shouted. "What are you doing here!" Later she said that for a split second she wondered if they jumped through the computer screen or something. Of course after this the Skype video call was ignored, but I could still watch what was happening. About a minute later my dad and JJ showed up, also looking surprised, but

Above: Shane and Donavon.
Right: Boiling the bear head to clean it up. Henry Swarey called me (he visited us last year), and I mentioned I was boiling a bear head on the kitchen stove. His response? "I bet Marlene is not at home right now."

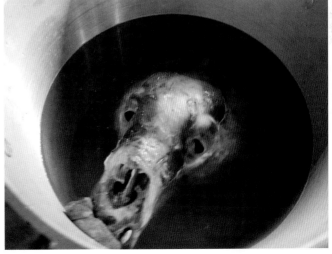

not to the extent my mom was. It was a good deal of fun. You never know when we might burst through a door somewhere. After all, Alaska is only 11 hours of travel from Pennsylvania. We drive that long for a good deal on groceries up North.

Next on the agenda was surprising the High family. This occurred the next day. It worked out better than I could have ever planned. Shane and Marlene were just going to walk into the hospital room and say hi. First, Marlene went over to their house and shocked Ann, who was at home. Then they headed into the hospital. As they were on the way in I got a call from Shannon. "Donovan would like to talk to Shane," he said. I explained that I was sorry, but Marlene and Shane weren't home at the moment. I didn't explain that they were really far from home at the moment. I told Shannon I would let Shane know, and he would talk to Donovan a bit later. This satisfied him, and we talked about the weather or something a bit and that was that.

Shannon and Donovan were startled when less than thirty minutes later Shane and Marlene strolled into the hospital room. "I heard you wanted to talk to me," Shane told Donovan. "Wait, how is that possible?" said Shannon. I wished I could be there with the rest of the family, but it was nice Shane and Marlene could go at least.

Marlene, Shane, and Dallas on the airplane heading to or from Pennsylvania. Judging from Marlene's stressed appearance (in the right photo) I am guessing they were traveling awhile.

Chapter 53
The *Doesn't Leak* Rides Again

This chapter title may be misleading, as I don't know if the *Doesn't Leak* had ever ridden anywhere in the past, beside to the boat shop. Readers may remember the hideous monstrosity of a boat that I hauled to Alaska in Book 3. My theory was that boats sell for a lot more in Alaska than they do in Pennsylvania. Yes, they do sell for more, but only if they are not oversized pieces of junk. That discovery was depressing, to say the least. For the past two years this boat (named the *Doesn't Leak*) sat around like a giant, ugly, 28 foot long lawn ornament, disrupting what would be an otherwise flawless state of matrimony. With Marlene out of town, I figured it would be a good time to at least try and put it on the water.

I called Paul, and he enthusiastically agreed to help me try a first actual voyage with the boat. We had tried at least three times before to take the boat out over the years, but they always ended in failure. It had always been typical problems common to boating, such as the key didn't work, the boat didn't want to shift into reverse, or the engine threw a rod. While I didn't suspect this time would be any different it was at least worth a try. Besides I was trying to sell the boat, and pictures of it on the water would certainly make the advertisement more attractive.

Because nothing on the *Big Ugly* (as we came to call it) was Coast Guard compliant, we decided to launch the boat at Skilak Lake. Because this is a fresh water lake it only falls under Fish and Game regulations. We probably broke a bunch of those rules as well, but Fish and Game are nicer to talk to than the Coast Guard. I had never noticed any large boats on Skilak Lake, and we soon discovered why.

We backed the *Big Ugly* down into the water and discovered the boat ramp had been made for tiny, midget-sized boats. I tried to ignore several people that walked over and appeared to be gawking like they had never seen a boat before. The tail of Paul's Suburban hung way down into the water, and I still could not budge the boat from the trailer. "Back up further," I yelled to Paul. He made motions that seemed to indicate he didn't want water running through the back of his Suburban. "It's only freshwater!" I yelled. Saltwater will destroy a vehicle quickly, but freshwater is harmless. Paul relented and backed up a little more. Bubbles were forming all around the back of his Suburban. I shifted the boat into reverse and gunned it. Finally, ever so slowly, the boat started to pull off the trailer. Suddenly I wondered if this was a good idea. The boat weighed over 6,000 pounds. If it was this hard to unload, how would it be to load it back up? I quickly dismissed this negative thought from my mind and gave it full throttle.

Above: I never realized Paul's Suburban was so small.
Below: The boat actually works! Who would ever believe it?

The boat eased completely off the trailer. I was speechless. Over the years, in my mind, the boat had ceased to become a boat. Taking it out was something we talked about, but never really planned to do. It felt like I was taking a gazebo or some other landscaping decoration out for a spin. But it did seem to float. While Paul took the Suburban around to park I tentatively turned the *Doesn't Leak* out to deeper waters and gave it some throttle. The boat certainly wasn't an 18 footer, that was for sure. It felt like a school bus was sticking out in front of me. Cautiously I headed back into shore to pick Paul up. I knew I would probably over estimate something, ram the shore, and pierce the hull on the many rocks there. The boat would sink, and I would get all kinds of letters from Fish and Game demanding I remove my boat from their lake.

Thankfully picking Paul up was fairly uneventful. He did have a hard time climbing up over the nose, but somehow he managed it. I had not wanted to back into shore, because I was worried I would hit the prop. Navigating this huge lug was much harder than my other boat. For some reason we also brought Mary Kate, Landon, and Kirk along. They had a great time running around in the galley and would have certainly jumped overboard had we not restrained them.

As we chugged around the lake I turned on the ancient fish finder. It looked like something that would belong in a museum, and I seriously doubted it would work. It actually powered up and showed us depths and what it claimed were fish. Just between me and you readers, I don't think it could tell a fish from a rusty tin can.

The shores of Skilak Lake can be rocky. Not wanting to try to swim in 50 degree water we stayed out towards the middle. We opened the engine up and were disappointed that we could only hit 25 mph. I guess that is not bad for such a big boat, but I was hoping to go faster. Driving the boat was an experience. It was more like driving a motorhome after spending all your time in a car.

After about thirty minutes of cruising, the engine started to falter at full throttle. We quickly turned around and headed back, as we had no kicker motor along. The faltering got worse and worse, until we could only go about 10 mph. Later we discovered the issue had been carb ice. This can occur in almost any temperature, as the effect of the gasoline turning to vapor in the carburetor has the same cooling effect similar to releasing propane from a bottle. At the time I just figured the boat was throwing another fit, and we would probably lose the engine.

The boat kept going, and we returned back to the dock. Surprised to have made it back, we drove in giant circles to see if it would keep running. The lake was calm as glass which dismayed me. I wanted to see how such a boat would handle waves. Paul took the boat in circles as fast as we could to

Above: Mary Kate and Kirk enjoyed the ride immensely.

Below: The galley of the *Doesn't Leak*. It is like a small RV, complete with a table, bench, and two beds. There is even a sink and an oven. To the side is a bathroom. It has a heater plumbed into the engine, similar to a car heater. You can really warm it up, which would be handy for cold nights halibut fishing. Too bad I'm going to sell it.

generate waves, and then we attempted to ride the wakes. The wakes did not seem to phase the boat. Here I noticed more annoying people gathering on the shore to stare at us. It's a lake, hello. You're supposed to use boats on it!

Finally the dreaded time came to load the beast back on the trailer. Once again I nervously got close to shore, and Paul leaped off into waist deep water. He was just as worried as I was about impaling the boat on rocks. I nervously drummed my fingers on the steering wheel as I waited on the boat for Paul to return with the Suburban and trailer. Mentally I tried to will away the onlookers who had nothing to do but wander around on the shore and cast glances our way. My telepathic messages failed miserably.

Paul backed the trailer in, and I tried to drive the boat onto it. The first attempt failed miserably, and I backed up. I was worried if I gave it too much gas I would go crooked on the trailer, miss the stop on the boat trailer and crash into the Suburban. Paul backed up a bit further in the water, but not as far as he had when we unloaded. Again I lined up and goosed the throttle. The last thing that I expected to happen did. Smooth as butter the boat slid up onto the trailer, the bow coming within six inches of the rubber stop. Success! I told Paul to go ahead and pull the trailer up and out of the water.

Here I discovered another issue with large boats. With my 18 foot aluminum boat you can move it around on the trailer, after you pull it out of the water. Not so with the *Big Ugly*. I figured I could winch it the last six inches to the rubber stop, but it wouldn't budge. So we had to back in one last time, until it was floating a bit. Then it was no problem to winch it up the last few inches. Elated and excited, we loaded the children up and headed for home. Later Marlene was unimpressed that we took the boat out, despite showing her all the great pictures we got of it. With pictures like that, selling the boat should be a breeze! Who knows, maybe it would sell even better with additional pictures on the salt water and some halibut laying about.

Chapter 54
The 3D Printer

While Marlene was in Pennsylvania I also ordered a 3D printer. This was not without her knowledge, as we did discuss it before she left. For years I have been intrigued and fascinated with 3D printers. These machines will take a 3D drawing and actually create a physical object with plastic! They do it one layer at a time. A three inch tall bear statue might have a few hundred layers in it. This means they are also very slow at making anything.

Three or four years ago when I noticed the falling price of 3D printers I excitedly called my dad and told him how cheap they had become. Our business should buy one! He asked what we would do with one, and I replied that I didn't know, but wouldn't it be ever so cool to have one? He disapproved of just buying random equipment because it was neat, and the idea fell by the wayside. But as time progressed they dropped even further in price.

Finally, I came up with a useful function for having a 3D printer. We could create giveaway items at trade shows. Instead of buying those high priced pens, and stuff like that, we could simply crank out little statues, key chains, or whatever to give away. We would no longer be at the mercy of the monopolists who sell trade show things. With that, it was settled, and the 3D printer was ordered. With one click of a button we would be over flowing with fancy goodies, customer goodwill would skyrocket, and all would be well.

After the printer arrived I discovered they were a bit harder to use than expected. It seems they love to jam up. You start a print, all looks well, and you turn your back. When you return, instead of a nice little dog bone there is a big pile of stringy plastic! Not many people are impressed by free piles of stringy plastic, so I resolved to tame the machine.

The first item I managed to successfully print for trade shows was hand spinners. These are basically a knockoff of the "fidget spinners". They are shaped like a dog bone with our business name and have a bearing in the middle. You can sit there for hours and spin them on your finger. They are not very practical, but people seem to really like them. Maybe it's just because they are free.

I also discovered I could download an endless amount of 3D models and print them. For example I needed a lemon juicer. Rather than go spend a fortune for some high priced lemon juicer I just downloaded one and printed it. I couldn't help but feel smart doing that.

Another big idea was to 3D print our Eskimo Checkers game. I figured we could just line up a bunch of these 3D printers and have a production line like Henry Ford in 1924. Our basement would turn into a virtual production line, and we would crank out pallets of the games. Unfortunately I discovered that the machines are so slow at printing the games that electric usage plays a significant role in the price of production. They also make so much heat that a couple of them can render a room unbearable. The small fact nobody bought the plastic games but instead preferred the quality wooden ones Ethan made, had a serious negative effect on production. I also made up a game called "Roadwork". Unfortunately that also went over like a lead balloon. It's good we are better at making books than games (or at least I hope we are).

A special thanks to Joel Telling, the 3D Printing Nerd, or so he calls himself online. He has many helpful tutorial videos about 3D printing. His website is www.The3DPrintingNerd.com. The instructional videos he produces are very clean and professional (and also funny).

Below: The 3D printer prints a lemon juicer. I imagine I will eventually save a fortune by not having to purchase lemon juicers.

Chapter 55
The Alaska State Fair

Marlene, Dallas, and Shane returned in time for a visit to the Alaska State Fair. I know some folks are opposed to going to fairs, so I apologize if it offends anyone. The Alaska State Fair is more of an agricultural event than a huge wild party. It attracts more than farmers though, as I never saw so many people with blue hair at one place before. What I really wanted to see were the massive pumpkins and squash that I have heard about. We were not disappointed.

After some careful thought we decided to just drive the motorhome. The fair was in Wasilla (no we didn't see Sarah Palin there) and is a good four hour drive from our place. We figured if we took the motorhome we could just stop and sleep if it got too late. We decided to go up on a Friday so we could also see the demolition derby. It had been years since I had been to one of those. So on Friday morning we headed north. On the way we swung into the Reinford's bakery and bought a few baked goods. Twila Reinford often gives us items that don't sell, and we decided it was only polite to actually buy a few things now and then.

The fair was noisy and overrun with people. I started to have second thoughts about being there, but we had driven four hours so it would have been a shame to just leave. After paying a premium for a parking space we marched everyone into the fairgrounds. Everyone was hungry and clamoring for food. I figured the cheapest thing to eat here would be hamburgers and French fries, so we found a trailer selling them. We dropped $70 on hamburgers and French fries! I was starting to see why some folks are opposed to visiting fairs. I may soon add my name to that list.

After eating the outrageously priced food, we headed over to the arena where the demolition derby was to take place. Anxiously we found some seats in the grandstands and waited. After what seemed like hours they finally announced the start of the demolition derby, which had a grand total of 14 cars! Last time I was at a demolition derby there were 100 or so. I guess small demolition derbies are just the price you have to pay to live in Alaska. In case you don't know what a demolition derby is, it is a contest where people drive cars into each other, and the one that stays moving the longest wins. Typically they use worn out old cars, and there are a bunch of rules to lower the chances of people getting hurt.

Watching the demolition derby made me think of our company cars. It seems someone is always running one through a ditch or finding a telephone pole to drive into. If a car happens to make it home unscathed, then rest assured some else will back into it. The rare few cars that don't get taken

Above: This pumpkin weighed 594 pounds.
Below: This pumpkin or squash, whatever it is, weighed 1,231 pounds. I would say those are respectable weights.

on off road joy rides or pole bending will inevitably have deer run out in front of them. There seems to be a direct correlation between the age of a car and the likelihood of it being in an accident. I'm thinking about buying some new cars, and then parking them in a bunker somewhere and letting them age about ten years. Then we could have the best of both worlds, vehicles that are reliable and also don't get wrecked every week. Once I got talked into buying a brand new Prius for the company. The car was wrecked at least three times in a year and a half, and it certainly wasn't because it had too much horsepower. The old hideous cars? I think you could drive them around Baghdad at night and be pretty safe.

After the demolition derby we went over to the produce competition. We were not disappointed with the size of the vegetables! One pumpkin weighed over 800 pounds. I wonder how they transport these things out of the fields. There were some enormous squash and carrots as well to look at. Alaska's long days more than compensate for the short growing season, and result in larger produce. There must be some tricks to the trade though as everything we tried to grow died in our garden. Actually our strawberries did ok, but the sweet corn only grew to be about eight inches tall.

We tried out a few of the rides, including the Ferris Wheel. It was ok; the children really enjoyed them. The rides were not super cheap, so everyone just got one ride, and then that was it for the evening. Everyone was tired out as we got back to the motorhome. I started up the rig, and turned the headlight switch on. To my dismay nothing happened! The lights were completely dead. It was late enough in the year that it now got dark, and there was no possible way to drive the four hours back in the dark. I was thankful we had our beds along. The next morning around six o'clock I fired up the motorhome and headed out of Wasilla while everyone else slept.

Chapter 56
Caribou Hunting With Marlene

Marlene was startled to discover earlier in the year that she had been selected for a caribou draw tag. She claimed she was sure she had not entered her name, in fact she didn't even know such a thing existed (the draw tag, not caribou). I calmed her fears and told her that perhaps it was a case of stolen identity, except in this case it was helpful. In fact she should avoid a victim mentality and actually use the tag for hunting, teaching whoever submitted her name a lesson.

The tag Marlene had been issued was good for the area around Skilak Lake. It also extended to some other areas. She decided it wouldn't hurt if I took her on a boat ride around Skilak Lake to scout for some caribou and check the area out.

One afternoon in early September we headed back to Skilak Lake with our blue van (not the bullet hole one) and our 18 foot boat. I knew better than to try to launch the 28 footer again, and besides, Marlene harbored a deep loathing for it. The big ugly boat was better off somewhere else. On the road into Skilak Lake the van started making some terrible grinding noises.

Occasionally my vans lose wheel bearings, which is not a problem. They often will go hundreds of miles making scraping noises before totally failing. This particular noise grew louder by the foot. I started to wonder if we could even make it to the lake. Not making it would be a tragedy! I pushed the van harder, trying to ignore the screams of tortured metal.

Thankfully the van made it the final few feet to the boat launch ramp. I loosened the straps and backed it in. It only took a few minutes to slide the boat off, and then Marlene pulled the van around to a parking spot. By now the van was going clank-clank-clank instead of just making grinding noises. Brake fluid was also running out of the left front wheel area. I suspected something had seriously gone amiss. Talk about timing! What if it had occurred five miles away? We could have never pulled the boat that far by hand.

Marlene and I cruised around the sides of the lake. Skilak has some rocky shoals here and there, and I didn't want to nail any. We got a close look at Caribou Island, which has several cabins on it. After that we cruised down towards the end of the lake with the glacier. Parts of the lake was hundreds of feet deep, and then it would abruptly change to twenty feet. I wished that I had brought some fishing rods along.

After an hour or two it was time to head back. We decided that we would again return, but with more time. Just a short evening out on the water was not long enough. Thankfully I had phone service, so I just called Paul

Above: Skilak Lake at dusk. It was very calm that evening.
Below: Being glacier fed, Skilak Lake has a deep green color.

and begged him to come help me out. He relented, and I promised to return the favor by loaning him the boat sometime. Paul also took us all home, along with the boat. We left the blue van sit at Skilak Lake and hoped some-one would steal it.

A few days later we returned again. Marlene's sister, Jo, had again agreed to watch the children for the whole day. We brought lunch along and some fire starter. There was a nifty little beach that we wanted to tie the boat off and make a small campfire and grill our food. But first we were going to boat around the lake looking for caribou. I realize that it is unlikely to find a caribou calmly standing at the lake shore, but you never know. It was worth a try at least.

We slowly cruised around a point, about halfway down the lake. To our shock, a huge black bear lumbered along the shore. He was definitely the largest black bear I have ever seen. I motioned for Marlene, so she saw the bear (or possibly she saw it first and motioned to me), and I killed the boat motor and let the boat drift towards the bear. This bear was as good as dead! My .300 Winchester Magnum could easily shoot 300 yards, and the bear was only about one hundred yards away. As soon as I put the scope on the bear I realized I had a problem. The waves were a bit choppy, and I couldn't hold the gun steady. Trying to rest off the bow of the boat made it even worse! In hindsight I should have carefully started the motor and tried to slowly get closer to the bear. But instead I held the gun as steady as I could and pulled the trigger. A huge geyser of sand exploded directly from the bank directly behind the bear.

Bears look like big, slow clumsy things incapable of doing anything fast. That is until you shoot at one and miss. This bear took off like a rocket, paws clawing the ground, sand spraying in all directions. He was gone before I could reload. Just in the unlikely case of a hit, we motored the boat in and tied it off on the beach. Indeed, the bear was gone, with only tracks in the sand. At least it was a clean miss, and I didn't have to worry about following a wounded bear around the woods.

We had an enjoyable dinner over a campfire on the sandy beach, and then continued motoring around the shore line. Despite not shooting any-thing, we had a good time. There were plenty of birds to see, including sever-al bald eagles. That afternoon we loaded up the boat. We were done hunting caribou for that day, but not done for the year. In fact we were just getting started. Stay tuned...

The Limo visits Perry View School in Landisburg, Pennsyvalnia. (April, 2017)
Would your school be interested in having the Snader Family visit and talk about Alaska?
Email us at TheSnaders@gmail.com and we will see what we can do. (And it's free.)

Notes on this book and the next one

Usually when I'm tying up a book I am dismayed over things that were not included. This book is no exception. I wanted to include more about our many visitors that stopped in, Kenny and Teresa Fox, Al and Verna Beiler, and many more.

The cabin rentals in Anchor Point had a rocky start. We did rent them out a few times, but we did not feel ready. Our first renters commented that the bulldozer in the front yard was a nice touch. He appreciated the fact we told him to just go ahead and re-landscape anything he didn't like. The cabins will be for rent again in 2018, although probably without the bulldozer.

A good bit of our next book (Book 7) is already written, however the title has not been decided yet. I doubt there will be as long a lag between Book 6 and 7 as there was with some of the other books. In the fall of 2017 we went hunting several times for caribou, including one fly-in hunt on a float plane. A big shocker was when Marlene started taking flight lessons. I'm taking lessons as well, but I doubt very many readers will find that terribly surprising. Oddly, Marlene likes flying more than I do.

In December of 2017 we also went deer hunting. We spent about one week on Kodiak Island, and another week in the little remote town of Cordova. It was a lot of fun and pretty eventful. For the Cordova trip we took my small boat over on the ferry and hunted out of that. I may compile the deer hunts in a separate book. We'll see how it goes.

As I was finishing everything up in this current book I got a call about Calvin Martin (he flew up to help Jesse Stauffer with my house flooring). He was killed in a tragic traffic accident in Union County, Pennsylvania on January 4, 2018 . The next book will have a lot about Calvin, and this was a real blow. The last part of 2017 he spent about six weeks in Alaska helping me build a cabin. I got to know him very well, and he was excited about returning in the summer of 2018. A few days before he flew home in late November we went out fishing. We didn't catch much of anything, but we got into a pod of Orcas. They were literally twenty or thirty feet from the boat, and it was amazing. That day will always be a special memory for me. How short life is; value every moment.

Until the next book,
Matt Snader

Map of Alaska

It is helpful to know where the towns and cities are that Matt talks about in his books. Here is a quick map to help you get a basic idea of Alaskan geography.

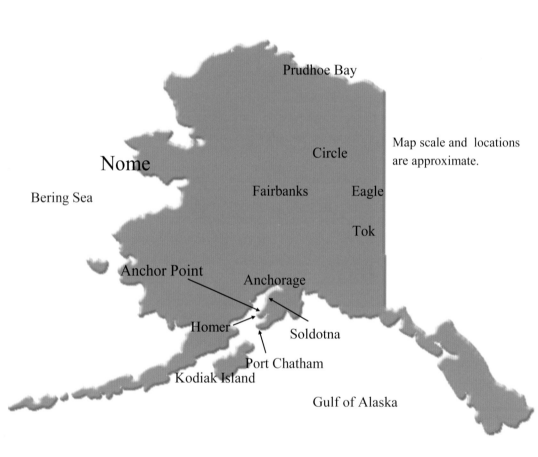

Prudhoe Bay

Circle

Map scale and locations are approximate.

Nome

Bering Sea

Fairbanks

Eagle

Tok

Anchor Point

Anchorage

Homer

Soldotna

Port Chatham

Kodiak Island

Gulf of Alaska

You may have noticed I no longer write blog updates on our website. That is because I now write for various publications, and I simply run out of time to write each month. The following two publications I write articles for regularly, so if you enjoyed the blogs, or can't wait for the next book to come out, consider subscribing to these papers. If you own a business you may want to consider placing ads in these publications as well. I advertise our books in both and have been very pleased with the results. A little bit of bragging-the cover photo of the bear in the Jan-Feb 2017 Hometown Outdoors comes from the game camera on my lane in Alaska. You will regularly find Alaska wildlife and pictures from my camera in both publications listed here. Hometown Outdoors is now a monthly publication, so contact them for current rates. And tell them Matt Snader sent you when you call or write them. No, I don't get a commission, but it does make me feel useful.

Plain Communities Business Exchange (PCBE) is a monthly newspaper/magazine featuring stories about manufacturing, farming, and many other subjects among the plain people. Each month we have theme based stories, with most of these being written by people with an inside view of the Amish Mennonite culture.

We have some great writers that are continually submitting stories on how to start new businesses, manage cash flow, banking, employee relations and many more. For your subscription, click on the link below or send a check to PCBE, PO Box 520, Millersburg PA 17061. Cost is $17.00 for 1 year (12 copies) mailed to your address.